Human Rights for OCR and Ec
with an introduction to the nature of substantive la

(the English legal system and the nature of law)
Sally Russell LLB (Hons), PGCE
Key features

Tasks and self-test questions throughout (with answers at www.drsr.org)

Key cases highlighted

Examples to bring the law to life

Links between the law and the English legal system / nature of law

Summaries with diagrams for the main points of each area

Examination pointers

Examination guidance and question practice

My main objective has been to combine legal accuracy with a style that is accessible to all students, so I hope you will find this book both stimulating and helpful. Fully updated with recent cases and laws it is written in a lively, clear and accessible way and is designed to help students of all learning styles to understand the subject.

Other books by Sally Russell

As new books may be available by the time you read this I have not listed my other books by title. They currently include crime and tort at AS and A2 level for both the AQA and OCR examination boards and the nature of law for AQA, OCR and Eduqas. Also *'the law explained'* series offers a more in-depth coverage of individual areas with additional tasks, examples and examination practice. These cover much of crime and tort as well as the various concepts of law. This means you can pick those topics for which you need more guidance (all the answers to tasks are included in the booklets).

For the most up-to-date list of what is available please check my author's page on Amazon or visit my website at www.drsr.org. All my books are available in both Kindle and paperback

©Copyright Sally Russell 2018. All rights reserved.

Table of contents

Table of contents	2
Introduction: things you need to know and links to other areas	5
More on how the key features can help:	5
Introduction to human rights law	7
Chapter 1 Rules and theory in human rights law	9
The nature of law	9
Legal rules and liability	9
The theory and nature of law for A-level	9
The rule of law	15
The theory of human rights: what is a right?	17
Interests: claim rights and residual freedoms	17
Fundamental rights	19
Chapter 2 A brief history of the development of human rights in Europe	20
Human rights in international law	20
The Second World War and its aftermath	20
The United Nations and the Universal Declaration of Human Rights 1948	20
The Council of Europe and the ECHR	20
Human rights in the UK before the Human Rights Act 1998 (HRA)	22
Magna Carta, the Bill of Rights and the rule of law	22
Status of the ECHR in the UK and the impact of decisions of the ECtHR	24
Human rights in the UK after the Human Rights Act 1998	26
Incorporation and interpretation of the ECHR	27
Impact of decisions of the ECtHR on the UK	31
Criticisms and reform of human rights – see Chapter 7	33
Chapter 3 Rights and restrictions under Articles 5 and 6 of the ECHR	35
The right to liberty under Article 5	35
What is deprivation of liberty?	36
Restrictions on the right to liberty under the ECHR	38
Provisions in English law which impact on the right to liberty	40
Police powers under PACE, SOCPA and CJPOA	41
Breach of the peace	44
Derogation and A 5 (3)	46

The right to a fair hearing under Article 6	*49*
Restrictions on Article 6 and the impact of English law provisions	*51*

Chapter 4 Rights and restrictions under Articles 8, 10 and 11 of the ECHR — 54

The right to respect for private and family life under Article 8 — *54*
    What is the right to a private and family life? — 54
    Restrictions on A 8 — 57

The right to freedom of expression under Article 10 — *57*
    What is freedom of expression? — 58
    Restrictions on A 10 — 59

The right to freedom of peaceful assembly and association under Article 11 — *60*
    What is freedom of assembly and association? — 60
    Restrictions on A 11 — 61
    The margin of appreciation in all three qualified rights — 62
    Legality, proportionality and legitimate aims — 63

Chapter 5 Provisions of English law which impact on Articles 8 10 and 11 — 67

Provisions in English law which impact on the rights under A 8 — *68*
    Interception of communications, data collection and retention — 68
    Surveillance and other police powers — 69
    Breach of confidence and misuse of private information — 70
    Defamation — 72
    Harassment — 73
    Other provisions — 74

Provisions in English law which impact on the rights under A 10 — *75*
    Freedom of Information and data protection — 75
    Defamation, breach of confidence, contempt of court, official secrets and trespass — 77
    Obscenity, racial hatred, censorship and blasphemy — 78
    Police powers and breach of the peace — 80

Provisions in English law which impact on the rights under A 11 — *81*
    Obstruction of the highway — 82
    Breach of the peace — 82
    The Public Order Act 1986 (POA) — 83

Chapter 6 Balancing the rights and enforcement — 87

Balancing the rights — *87*

Enforcement of human rights — *92*

Claims before the ECtHR — *93*
    The effect of a successful case in the ECtHR on the state and claimant — 94

Claims in the domestic courts — *94*
    The effect of a decision in the UK courts on the state and claimant — 97

Claims by way of judicial review	*98*
The effect of judicial review decisions on the state and claimant	99
Chapter 7 criticisms of human rights in the UK and proposals for reform	**101**
Overview	*101*
Criticisms of the ECHR and ECtHR	*102*
Criticisms of the HRA	*104*
Proposals for reform	*105*
A Bill of Rights – the past and the future	106
Arguments for a Bill of Rights	107
Arguments against a Bill of Rights	107
Conclusion	108
Chapter 8 Revision and examination practice	**110**
Revision	*110*
Examination guidance	*115*
Application advice	115
Evaluation advice	117
Extract from Human Rights for AQA A Level Law on links to the nature of law	*119*
Examination question practice	*125*
Index of cases	**126**

 *Introduction: things you need to know and links to other areas*

This book covers human rights law for OCR and Eduqas, as well as an introduction to the nature of law.

More on how the key features can help:

Examples help you to see how the law relates to real life situations

Key cases show you the important cases to know, and where a principle of law is established this is clearly stated

Tasks and self-test questions help you to check your understanding

Examination pointers help with application

Evaluation pointers help you to see problems with the law. These may relate to the development and reform of the law as well as to the rule of law and justice (both of which require fairness and clarity)

Summaries and diagrams help to make the law clear and accessible

Links between human rights and the English legal system / nature of law show you how to connect these using examples from this topic

There are only a few 'key cases' in this book because most are of equal value. However, I have highlighted one or two which have had the most impact on the law or on public opinion.

It is a bit early to talk about examinations but there are a couple of things you need to know now so you can use the book effectively.

In some questions you will be asked to apply the law to a set of facts, in others to evaluate it. There are 'pointers' throughout the book to help with this.

Examination pointers

These relate to legal rules and application of the law. For application of the law you need to identify the specific legal rules that apply to the given facts. Then you need to apply those rules logically to the facts in order to reach a sustainable conclusion. You will need to support what you say by using cases and principles to illustrate your points and then reach a conclusion based on your application.

The law for application is the current law and latest case developments.

Evaluation pointers

These cover criticisms of the law. They are for evaluation questions where you may be asked to provide a critique of the law on a particular topic or a particular legal rule. Any problems with the law will also suggest that the rule of law is not being upheld or justice not achieved as both these concepts require fairness and clarity. The evaluation pointer may show the law has improved in some way, too, as any critique should include the good points. The law for evaluation may need to include developments or advantages and disadvantages, not just the latest cases and principles.

Try to produce a balanced argument. Where there is debate on an issue there are usually valid arguments on both sides, so don't strive to write what you think examiners want to see; they will be much more impressed by independent thought. Have an opinion, but look at the issue from the other point of view too to show that you have considered the arguments before reaching that opinion.

As Chapter 7 is devoted to evaluation there are not so many of these pointers along the way as usual.

A final few things before you start the book.

It is important to try to learn plenty of cases as these help to show you how the law works in practice. If you have trouble remembering the names, then do the best you can, but be sure that you can support any application or evaluation with examples.

Criminal cases are usually in the form *R v the defendant (D)* e.g., R v Smith. These are usually abbreviated to just Smith in textbooks and you may do so too.

Civil cases are between the *claimant* (C) and the *defendant* (D), e.g., Smith v Jones 2017, although you will still see the use of the old word *plaintiff* in cases before 1999, when it changed to *claimant*.

Judicial review cases are used quite a bit in human rights law. These are an application to a court to challenge the legality of state decisions or use of powers which infringe certain rights. They are in the form *R (on the application of the Smith) v the government department* (or other body against whom the case is brought). The part in brackets 'on the application of Smith' means that Smith is the person applying for a review of the law. Again these can be abbreviated to Smith.

Human rights cases may be ordinary court cases or by way of judicial review in the national court, as above. However if the case is taken to the European Court of Human Rights it is in the form *Smith v UK*.

There is a list of some common abbreviations in the appendix at the end of the book.

Introduction to human rights law

The **European Convention on Human Rights** (**ECHR**) is formally called the Convention for the Protection of Human Rights and Fundamental Freedoms. It provides for human rights to be protected in the states which sign up to it.

Convention rights have been the subject of many cases which involve a balance of the interests of the individual against those of the state. Some of the rights also conflict with each other such as freedom of expression and the right to a private life. We will look at examples as we go through the different rights, expressed in the **ECHR** as Article numbers.

Under the **ECHR**, **Article 1** obliges all signatories to secure the rights and freedoms contained in it for those within their jurisdiction. Originally, it set out 13 rights, under **Articles 2** to **14**. Since 1950 the rights in the original document have been added to by various protocols over the years. Protocols are not usually compulsory so are only binding on those who have agreed to them. The UK has not signed up to most of these.

Convention rights have been the subject of many cases which involve a balance of the interests of the individual against those of the state. Some of the rights also conflict with each other such as freedom of expression and the right to a private life. We will look at examples as we go through the different rights, expressed in the **ECHR** as Article numbers.

Under the **ECHR**, **Article 1** obliges all signatories to secure the rights and freedoms contained in it for those within their jurisdiction. Originally, it set out 13 rights, under **Articles 2** to **14**. Since 1950 the rights in the original document have been added to by various protocols over the years. Protocols are not usually compulsory so are only binding on those who have agreed to them. The UK has not signed up to most of these.

Examination pointer

This book covers the law for OCR and Eduqas.

The specifications require knowledge of Articles 5, 6, 8, 10 and 11

Article 15 allows governments to derogate from (avoid) these rights in certain situations so is a restriction on human rights. There are plenty of other restrictions both within the specific Articles and within national laws and rules of procedure (such as police powers to deprive someone of the right to liberty). Restrictions of all types are discussed with each article rather than as a separate chapter because it is easier to understand the restrictions on a right while considering the right itself.

The five articles together with restrictions and enforcement are the main area of study for the OCR and Eduqas A-level specifications. However, you also need to have some knowledge of the rules and theory of human rights as well as its history and the impact the **Human Rights act 1998**. Finally, you should be able to offer a critique of human rights law along with ideas for reform. Here is how this book deals with these requirements.

Chapter 1 covers some general rules and principles relating to various rights and the basic theory of what rights are.

Chapter 2 covers a brief history of human rights and human rights in the UK before and after the **Human Rights Act 1998 (HRA)**.

The next two chapters cover the specific rights given in the **ECHR** as far as they are included in the OCR and Eduqas specifications, and the restrictions on these rights. Provisions of English law which impact on the rights are discussed in Chapter 5. These include areas of criminal law (e.g., the law on murder) and tort (e.g., defamation and harassment).

In Chapter 6 we look at how the different rights need to be balanced and enforcement of human rights both in domestic courts and at the European Court of Human Rights in Strasbourg. Criticisms and reform of human rights law, specifically in the UK, and the idea of another Bill of Rights for the UK are covered in Chapter 7.

Finally, the last chapter provides revision of what you have studied followed by examination guidance and practice.

In what follows I quote from the European Convention on Human Rights. This is available as a PDF document from the website of the European Court of Human Rights. You may find it helpful to have a copy at your elbow to refer to. The website also has some useful information and full judgements.

The home page is at https://www.echr.coe.int

For the PDF document click on "Official texts".

For cases click on "Case law" then "HUDOC database" and "Lists of judgments, decisions, advisory opinions". This provides an alphabetical list of all judgments which you can scroll through. Note however, that if you search by case name you need the full name.

For anything else, browse at will.

Chapter 1 Rules and theory in human rights law

This chapter covers an introduction to the nature of law, the rule of law and the theory of rights. The first two are covered in my other books but provide the background to all law, so are repeated here.

The nature of law

The nature of law is essentially that it is based on rules. Legal liability occurs when the rules have been broken. In order to understand the nature of law we need to know a bit more about where the law comes from, what distinguishes a legal rule from other rules (or norms) of behaviour, how a person may become liable in law and what differences there are between civil and criminal liability.

Sources of Law include the courts, which produce common law through cases heard in court, and Parliament which produces statute law. Some (not many) laws come from custom, i.e., they have been going on for so long they are accepted as law even though not set out in a case or statute. Other sources of law today include European law and Human rights law.

Legal rules and liability

There is no agreed definition of law. Essentially it is a matter of rules, but so is much a life. Therefore, a distinction needs to be made between enforceable legal rules and other norms of behaviour. There are many rules governing our lives but not all are enforceable. There may be rules governing how you behave in school or college, and there will be rules at home too. None of these rules have the force of law. A teacher or parent may punish (sanction) you for breaking these rules but there will be no such sanctions from a court of law.

Law is based on liability. A person is legally liable when accountable in law for something done/not done. There are two types of liability, criminal and civil. Both are based on the principle of individuals being responsible for their conduct.

- **Criminal liability is based on an individual's responsibility to the state and society as a whole**
- **Civil liability is based on an individual's responsibility to other individuals**

The theory and nature of law for A-level

The nature of law not only covers what law is and where it comes from, as well as the differences between civil and criminal law, but also includes how law operates in society, involving different theories (or concepts) of law which are studied for the full A-level. These are covered in depth in my book "The Nature of Law for OCR A Level", as legal theory is a subject in its own right. The theories and concepts of law need to be related to all your other areas of study (i.e., they are synoptic). When considering the nature of law you need to look at the rest of your course from a different perspective. You should be able to use the substantive law to illustrate the concepts, and discuss the concepts in the context of the substantive law. It is therefore a good idea to think about them, at least briefly, as you work through the rest of your studies, so I have included a short introduction here to the main concepts.

The word law in phrases such as criminal law, human rights law, contract law etc., refers to the substance of the law (hence these topics are called substantive law). The word law in a wider sense is a more elusive concept, as it relates to the nature rather than the substance of law. It involves consideration of what academics and judges think the nature of law is (and what it should be). This in itself involves consideration of theories of law, such as law and justice, law and morality, the role of law in balancing competing interests and the role of law in punishing (criminal liability) or compensating (civil liability) based on fault.

Unlike AQA, OCR and Eduqas do not have specific linked questions. However, you will need to be able to use human rights case (as well as crime and tort ones) to illustrate the nature of law and the theories, or concepts, which it embraces. You should therefore consider how these might apply in practice as you work through your course. Thus, if you see a case which you think was decided unfairly you can ask yourself whether the law is achieving justice, or whether the competing interests were balanced appropriately.

The law plays a role in society by regulating behaviour and establishing social control. It punishes those convicted of a crime and compensates the victims of any civil wrongdoing. It also facilitates (e.g., by giving powers to form contracts or get married) and protects (e.g., by laws against theft and violence, and consumer protection laws). The law plays an important role in society not only in providing justice but also in balancing competing interests (both public and private) in order to do so. It sometimes involves enforcing moral as well as legal rules, and legal liability usually relies on fault, e.g., one role of the law is to punish those found to be at fault, or blameworthy.

Most people recognise the role of law in punishing offenders in criminal cases, but the law has a less obvious role in many other areas. The following are all real cases and provide examples of the role that the law plays in society in relation to the above concepts. This covers a range so that you can get an idea of how the law in practice relates to the different theories.

Case	Brief facts	The nature and role of law
Brown 1994 (See Chapter 7)	A criminal case where serious injuries had occurred during consensual sado-masochistic sex in private. Those involved were convicted of grievous bodily harm. A controversial case because they were all adults and no-one was forced.	In balancing the interests the law included the public interest (what was best for society) and also thought the moral wrong should be punished (society needs protecting from violent behaviour, even in private).
Re A 2001	A hospital sought a court order to allow an operation on Siamese twins to separate them. The result would be that one twin would die but without the operation they both would.	In granting the order the law had balanced many different interests. This not only included the people concerned but the public interest. The morality of the action also affected the decision in court. This shows the difficulty for the courts as society is divided on such issues.
Miller v Jackson 1977	A woman wanted the court to award an injunction to stop cricket being played nearby because she often had cricket balls landing in her garden.	In balancing the interests the court included the public interest and thought society would not be best served by granting an injunction to stop the cricket. The injunction was refused.
Murray v Express Newspapers 2008	The author of the Harry Potter books, JK Rowling, brought a case on behalf of her young son against a photographic agency for publishing secretly taken photographs of him.	The court had to balance the interests of the agency in freedom of expression against the child's right to privacy. The balance came down in favour of the child's right, but the court made clear each case would depend on its own facts and the decision could be different with an adult. This shows that in balancing interests the law is also protecting the vulnerable (the child).
Gemmell & Richards 2003 (See Chapter 3)	Two boys set light to some papers outside the back of a shop. Several premises were badly damaged. They were convicted of recklessly causing criminal damage by fire (arson) because the risk of damage was obvious to a reasonable person. Their ages were therefore not taken into account.	In order to achieve justice the HL overruled an earlier law and decided a person required a greater level of fault in order to be guilty of a crime. Thus to prove recklessness it must be shown that D is aware of a risk, but deliberately goes ahead and takes it. This shows the importance of proving fault in criminal law.

Some knowledge of these concepts is useful so you can understand how you can use human rights cases to illustrate them. Here is a brief description of each with a couple of views and/or comments as a taster, using cases from the table above (which includes crime, tort and human rights cases).

Balancing competing interests

If one person has a right (an "interest") this often conflicts with the rights of another person, as in **Murray v Express Newspapers 2008** in the table. To decide whose rights are to be enforced the courts must balance the competing interests to arrive at a decision. The balance is not only between private interests (as in **Murray**) but may be between public and private (as in **Miller v Jackson 1977**). There may be several interests to balance, as in **Re A 2001**, and the court may find the balancing act difficult – but that is part of the role of law: to consider difficult issues and decide what the legal position should be.

One view (that of Roscoe Pound) regarding competing interests is that law is an engineering tool which can be used to balance the different interests in society to achieve social control. However, he believed that public interests should not be balanced against private ones because the public interest will always prevail. A case example is **Miller v Jackson** where she won her case but did not achieve the remedy she asked for because the public interest lay in refusing the injunction. Human rights law is all about balancing the competing interests of the individual claiming the right and the state or public authority that is interfering with that right.

When you look at the cases in each chapter consider what the interests involved are and how they conflict. Then consider whether the law achieved an appropriate balance (and therefore justice).

Fault

Both civil and criminal liability is based (usually) on fault, or to put it another way a person is not liable unless blameworthy. Fault is an indicator of blame so it justifies the imposition of liability. The level of blame, or fault, is different in criminal and civil law. Criminal law usually requires a fairly high level of fault before someone is found guilty of a crime, i.e., that they acted with either intention or recklessness (an example of the latter is **Gemmell & Richards 2003** above). For civil law the most common type of fault is negligence, which is a lower level of fault. In human rights law the fault aspect is mainly seen in the finding of a violation of a right or a declaration of incompatibility between English law and the right.

Morals

The law is only involved when someone breaks legal rules, not social (or moral) ones. However, legal rules and social rules share many characteristics. This is what law and morality is about: how far social and legal rules overlap and whether the law should be involved in moral issues. Sometimes the law must get involved because a moral issue comes up in court and such cases often involve human rights. Cases on assisted dying (**R (on the application of Pretty) v DPP 2002**) and withdrawal of life support (**Bland 1993**) illustrate this. Other human rights cases include the locking up of suspected terrorists without trial. This is state interference with the right to liberty and the courts must assess whether it is justified in the interests of security.

There has been much debate on the subject of law and morals and there are opposing views. Here are simplified versions of three:

Professor Hart says that law and morals are separate and the law should not be used to enforce morality. If a law is made using the proper procedures, it is a valid law even if immoral, and so it must be obeyed. This is positivism.

Lord Devlin said that law and morals are related and immoral acts, even in private, should be punished. Also, even if made using the proper procedures, if a law is immoral it is not a valid law and need not be obeyed. This is natural law.

John Stuart Mill said that the law shouldn't normally be used to enforce morality unless harm to others is involved. This is libertarianism; it is also a type of positivism based on utilitarianism (see under justice).

The decision in **Brown 1994** was partly based on the fact that the acts were seen as immoral. Hart would see that as irrelevant, Devlin would not. Mill might go either way as harm was caused to others but it was by consent. The decision was only by a 3-2 majority so you can see that the judges disagreed on this issue too. Note the overlap with justice. The three views above are all views on what justice involves.

We live in a pluralist society with diverse views, so there is no "shared morality". What some people see as immoral, others don't. This makes legal involvement in morals a tricky issue, especially in controversial areas like euthanasia, withdrawal or treatment or enforced feeding.

Justice

One important role of the law is to achieve justice, so any of the cases in the table can be used to illustrate this concept. The rule of law (see below) requires fairness, and this is one meaning of justice, as is equality, another part of the rule of law. However, justice means different things to different people and as you can see from **Re A 2001**, justice may be achieved for some but not all. There are different theories on what justice means and how it is achieved.

The three theories under law and morals are theories of justice. Another theory of justice, called utilitarianism, is that justice is achieved when the "*greatest happiness*" is achieved. A law which produces a lot of benefit would be a just law. Applying this to **Re A**, we can say that as the operation would save a life this was a big plus, so justice would be achieved by allowing it. However, if you look back to the natural law theory of justice, this is that it should have a moral content so an immoral law is not a proper law. On this view, the decision in **Re A** did not achieve justice because it was immoral to operate knowing the other twin would die. Utilitarianism looks at the greatest good overall and does not take account of individual rights. Perversely, this means it is particularly relevant in human rights law. This is because the courts must often balance individual rights against the public interest and a utilitarian view of justice would decree that the latter should prevail. A supporter of natural law would be more likely to support the individual right because most human rights are based on morality. When you look at different human rights cases consider whether the law achieves justice, and by whose theory.

Law and technology

Advances in technology have led to a great many human rights cases.

As technology develops and new technologies emerge the law must be prepared to keep up. Criminal examples are internet and email scams, online abuse and cyber-crime in general. Civil examples include data protection and advanced medical techniques which lead to disagreements as to whether a procedure is ethical. Both involve possible interference with human rights. Technological advances can lead to new procedures which haven't been possible before, e.g., cloning and tissue typing, and may need the intervention of the law in the case of disputes. Other examples are the use of drones and driverless cars, or robot-controlled procedures. Data protection and privacy are harder to control with such easy access to information through the internet and these are particularly relevant to human rights. There have been many human rights cases where individuals have challenged the state and the media over invasion of privacy, the first over surveillance and data collection and the second for spreading private information via social media and the internet.

The best way to see how the concepts apply in practice is by relating them to a case example. Here is an example of how all these theories can apply in a given situation. It is not an area you will study as it was a rape case, but it is an interesting example not only of the concepts, but also the English legal system (sources of law and influences on Parliament).

Example

R v R 1991, involved a man accused of raping his wife. They were separated and she had moved back in with her parents. He forced his way in to their house and assaulted her while attempting rape. At the time, rape within marriage was not against the law because a woman was deemed to have consented to sex purely by being married. The case went to the House of Lords (HL – now the Supreme Court) on appeal.

The HL decided that rape within marriage was no longer acceptable. The case is an example of the law needing to keep up with change, in this case changing social attitudes, but the same would apply to new technology. The judges presumably felt they achieved justice for the wife. Whether the man achieved justice is another matter. It is part of the concept of justice that the law is not retrospective and however wrong he may have been morally, at the time of the event his action was not against the law. In making the decision the court exercised a form of social control. In order to do this it had to balance the competing interests of D (not to be guilty of what had at the time been a legal act) against those of his wife (to have the law's protection) and the wider public interest (violence can affect society as a whole). The public interest will usually prevail and here there was the added interest of the wife. The fact that the act was accompanied by violence showed a greater degree of fault, which may have tipped the balance against D. He should be punished (sanctioned) for his wrongdoing and society should be controlled so that this type of behaviour is eradicated. Finally, there is clearly a moral issue because the judges thought the law was wrong to allow an immoral act such as rape, even within marriage. However, Hart (a positivist) could say the decision should be based only on legal rules not morality, and that D should not have been punished for what was at the time a legal action, even if it was immoral.

However, Devlin (a supporter of natural law) might agree that he should be punished because the law which allowed rape within marriage was itself immoral and so not valid.

It is also arguable that an elected Parliament should decide on whether this type of act is against the law, not unelected judges. In fact, Parliament did act, after the event, and changed the law to match the decision.

A utilitarian would say this decision, and the later law by Parliament, achieved justice as a greater number of people benefit from the law prohibiting acts of violence, especially as (unlike **Brown 1994**) it was against the victim's wishes.

As you work through this book and look at different cases, ask yourself the following questions.

- *Has justice been achieved?*
- *Does the law involve morality?*
- *What interests are competing and how has the law balanced them?*

Task 1 gives you an idea of how you might think about these concepts as you read a case.

Task 1

In **A v the Home Department 2005** several foreign nationals who were suspected of terrorism activities were held for three years without trial, The **Anti-terrorism, Crime and Security Act 2001** allowed the Home Secretary indefinitely to detain foreign nationals suspected of terrorism, without charge or trial.

The case went to the HL. The HL held the Act was against the rule of law and breached the right to liberty under the Convention.

What competing interests were balanced?

Do you think the decision achieved justice?

What role did morality play in the case?

In the above case, Lord Hoffman said that terrorism had succeeded if it meant the country rejected the rule of law in response to threats of terrorism. The rule of law inspires the whole legal system and is an important part of any law course. If you have already studied it, treat this next section as revision.

The rule of law

The preamble to the **Universal Declaration of Human Rights** says that if people are not to be compelled to rebel against tyranny and oppression that *"human rights should be protected by the rule of law"*. That was in 1948. In a 2014 lecture Lord Bingham included the protection of human rights as one of his eight sub-rules used to describe the rule of law in its current form. To those who have this from my other books please feel free to skip this section.

When rules of law and procedure are formulated they should conform to the rule of law. This involves equality, clarity and fairness.

- **The law should apply to everyone equally and no-one should be above the law.**

- **The law must be clear so that people know the rules (then if the rules are broken it will be fair to punish those at fault).**

- **The law must be accessible so that if a person is accused of a crime it is only fair that access to justice and legal advice is possible.**

This is a simplified description of the rule of law so needs further discussion.

The Rule of Law

The **Constitutional Reform Act 2005** refers to the rule of law, and the Lord Chancellor's oath requires the Lord Chancellor to respect the rule of law, but there is no agreed definition of it. An early view of the rule of law is that formulated by Dr Thomas Fuller in 1733: "Be you ever so high, the law is above you". This view has persisted for centuries. In **Evans v AG 2015**, the Supreme Court (SC) ruled that correspondence between Prince Charles and government ministers should be made public under the **Freedom of Information Act 2000** and said it was "fundamental to the rule of law" that decisions and actions of the executive are subject to review in a court of law.

The rule of law was popularised by A. V. Dicey (a constitutional lawyer) the following century who, in summary, said *"everyone, whatever his rank, is subject to the ordinary law of the land"*. A little more recently, Lord Bingham said *"If you maltreat a penguin in the London zoo, you do not escape prosecution because you are the Archbishop of Canterbury"*. So, an important part of the rule of law is that everyone is subject to it, with no exceptions. There is more to it than that, and opinions differ on what it means in the modern sense. Although the rule of law is a somewhat abstract notion, to try to explain it today, a good place to start is with Lord Bingham's 2014 lecture on the subject, taken from his book "The Rule of Law". The core principle is as above, that no-one is above the law, including those who make it. He notes that the rule of law has evolved and continues to do so, and sets out eight sub-rules which he feels describe the rule of law in its current form. These are:

Law must be accessible. This means that if people are bound by the law they must be able to know what the law is.

Questions of legal rights and liabilities should be resolved by application of the law and not be a matter of discretion. This does not mean there is absolutely no discretion. A judge must exercise a certain amount of discretion when deciding on an appropriate sentence or remedy – the point is that any such discretion is limited by law, e.g., statutes or earlier decisions.

The law should apply equally to all. This is accepted by most people as being part of any rule of law but Lord Bingham points out that in practice it is not always apparent. An example is the various **Terrorism Acts** where non-nationals suspected of terrorism are subject to being locked up without trial, but nationals are not – even though they pose the same threat. It is arguable that anyone subject to national laws should be entitled to the law's protection. In **R v Secretary of State for the Home Department Ex parte Kwawaja 1984**, Lord Scarman said *"He who is subject to English law is entitled to its protection"*. However, even where the law appears to apply equally it may not in practice. It is true that the Archbishop of Canterbury is not above the law – but if he does mistreat a penguin he can probably afford a decent lawyer to help his case! The **Legal Aid, Sentencing and Punishment of Offenders Act 2012 (LASPO)**, has severely reduced access to justice and legal aid, especially in civil cases.

The law should adequately protect fundamental human rights. This is perhaps a more recent addition to the concept of the rule of law. The preamble to the **Universal Declaration of Human Rights** says that if people are not to be compelled to rebel against tyranny and oppression that "human rights should be protected by the rule of law". Whilst acknowledging that there may be some disagreement as to what rights should be protected in different societies, Lord Bingham said that the rule of law required legal protection of such human rights as are seen within society as fundamental.

The state must meet its obligations under international law. Thus, an act by a state that is unlawful would be against the rule of law. He referred to the war against Iraq and while not saying whether or not he believed it to be illegal, he did say that if it *was* illegal then it would be against the rule of law "if this sub-rule is sound".

Means must be provided for resolving civil disputes. He says that if people are bound by the law they should receive its benefits and should be able to go to court to have their rights and liberties determined "in the last resort". He does not rule out less formal methods of resolving disputes but sees access to the courts as a "basic right" adding that legal advice should be affordable and available without excessive delay. Where the first sub-rule requires law to be accessible in the sense of clarity, this sub-rule requires accessibility in terms of cost. It has been said that justice is open to all "like the Ritz hotel" – meaning that everyone may be entitled to it but many are unable to use it in practice due to lack of money. Going back to the mistreatment of penguins, the Archbishop is more likely to be able to afford to go to the Ritz and to gain access to justice than the average person on the street is, especially since **LASPO**.

All public officials must exercise their power reasonably and not exceed its limits. As with the second rule, this rule is against the arbitrary use of power. An example of its application is that everyone has the right to apply for judicial review of a decision made by public officers and government ministers – a judge cannot overturn such a decision, but can rule that it is unreasonable.

Adjudicative procedures must be fair. This means open court hearings, the right to be heard, the right to know what the charges and evidence against you are, that the decision maker is independent and impartial, and that in criminal cases D is innocent until guilt is proved. Fairness would also cover access to justice in both the earlier senses of clarity and cost.

Lord Bingham sees the rule of law as depending on an unspoken bargain between the individual and the state. The citizen sacrifices some freedom by accepting legal constraints on certain activities, and the state sacrifices some power by recognising it cannot do all that it has the power to do. He concludes that this means those who maintain and protect the rule of law are "guardians of an all but sacred flame which animates and enlightens the society in which we live".

To sum up the rule of law:

- **No-one is above the law**
- **Everyone is subject to the law, not the arbitrary exercise of power**
- **The law must encompass clarity, access to justice, fairness and an independent and impartial judiciary**
- **The law must apply equally**

In Lord Bingham's view, the rule of law should also protect human rights and comply with international obligations if it is to apply to a modern state with national and international commitments. This is useful to include when illustrating and evaluating human rights. As you study the law try to consider whether the rule of law is being upheld.

The rule of law and human rights

The prevention of the arbitrary use of power by public officials underpins most of the rights in the **ECHR**. This means policies and decisions should not be indiscriminate. They should be properly thought out and regard should be paid to individual circumstances. Accessibility to the law through courts and tribunals is another requirement of both. In **R (Gillan) v Commissioner of Police of the Metropolis 2006**, Lord Bingham said that the exercise of power by public officials must not be used arbitrarily and that the law must be sufficiently accessible. The **ECHR** allows for some restrictions on rights, but only if they are in *"accordance with law"*. This concept would require any national policy or law to be compatible with the rule of law if the state is to avoid being in violation of a right.

Task 2

Explain what Lord Bingham meant when he said *"If you maltreat a penguin in the London zoo, you do not escape prosecution because you are the Archbishop of Canterbury"*. Add a comment of your own as to whether you agree that this should be part of the rule of law.

The theory of human rights: what is a right?

The following is taken from the chapter on balancing competing interests in my book on the nature of law.

Interests: claim rights and residual freedoms

An interest is similar to a right. With most rights come corresponding duties. Thus, in criminal and civil law we have a right not to be harmed. This imposes a corresponding duty on others not to cause harm, whether in criminal law or through negligence. In contract law we have a right to receive goods and a duty to pay the agreed price. The other party to the contract has a corresponding duty to supply the goods and a right to receive payment. In legal procedure there is a right to legal advice following an arrest and a corresponding duty to provide access to a solicitor. This correspondence principle was put forward by an American law professor, Wesley Hohfeld (1879 – 1918). He also noted that people, including lawyers, used the word "right" rather indiscriminately and attempted to clarify it by comparing rights to liberties (or freedoms). A right can be claimed and comes with a corresponding duty, as in the right to the contract price (Hohfeld referred to this as a claim right). A liberty is the freedom to do as you choose and this imposes no corresponding duty (this is a privilege not a right that can be claimed). We saw in Chapters 2 and 3 that Mill was a libertarian, so felt people should be free to choose how to act as long as it did not harm others. Only then should the law step in. His theory would prefer interests to be liberties rather than rights. That would give greater freedom of choice as it would not impose duties (other than the duty not to harm others). Rights can be claimed, liberties cannot.

Example

I have a right not to be harmed by someone's negligence and can claim that right. I can ask the law to enforce it by making a claim in court. I have a liberty to go to a pop concert, but I cannot claim it as a right if the concert is sold out and I can't get in. However, if I had a ticket this would give me a contractual right so I could claim this right and sue for breach of contract.

Some countries, such as America and Germany, have a constitution which gives rights. These are claim rights and are enforceable by law. Other countries, like the UK, have a system based on freedoms. The UK system means anything not specifically prohibited is allowed, but is not enforceable by law. So there are claim rights and residual freedoms, or liberties.

Example

There is a sign in the park saying, "No cycling". This is a rule (probably a council by-law) and if it is disobeyed the rule can be enforced by law, usually by imposing a fine.

There is no sign in the park. In Germany, this means you cannot cycle as there is no notice permitting it. In the UK, it means you can cycle; it is not forbidden so you are free to do it. This is a residual freedom; what is left after the law has regulated what you must or must not do. You cannot however, claim that you have a right to cycle.

There is a sign in the park saying "Cycling is permitted". This would be a claim right and enforceable by law. If someone tries to stop you cycling you can say "I have a right to cycle here".

UK citizens have some rights but these mostly come from international law, e.g., the rights from the **European Convention on Human Rights (ECHR)** which are part of UK law by way of the **Human Rights Act 1998 (HRA).** Other rights come under **The Charter of Fundamental Rights of the European Union**, at least for now.

Rights and freedoms (interests) often compete. I have a right to free speech but this is constrained by a person's right not to be defamed by untrue statements and by the right to privacy. My right to free speech also allows me to protest against unjust laws. If lots of people protest there may be a danger of disrupting public order. This is where the rights and freedoms may need balancing. In the first example, the law must balance freedom of speech against the right not to be defamed. In the second, it must balance the need for free speech in a democratic society against the need to maintain order to protect that society.

So the law protects people's rights by imposing a duty on others not to interfere with those rights. Whether making or enforcing the law, Parliament and the courts must balance people's rights and freedoms and try to satisfy as many interests as possible. Whether civil or criminal, all cases involve some kind of balancing process between the interests of the parties involved. Many cases also involve the wider public interest and the law will take this into account as well.

From The Nature of Law for OCR by Sally Russell

So you can see that this topic is strongly related to the concept of balancing competing interests. Think about this as you go through the book because it will give you a store of cases to use to illustrate that concept as well as human rights.

Fundamental rights

The **European Convention on Human Rights** (**ECHR**) is formally called the **Convention for the Protection of Human Rights and Fundamental Freedoms**. The formal name uses the term *"fundamental freedoms"* but the rights given under the **ECHR** are what Hohfeld called claim-rights. The **ECHR** gives the rights and imposes a corresponding duty on the state to guarantee them.

Other fundamental rights come from the European Union which has a Charter to protect a range of rights including all those contained in the **ECHR**. This is the **Charter of Fundamental Rights of the Union** (known as the EU Charter). It was proclaimed in Nice in 2000, but has only been legally binding since the **Lisbon Treaty** came into force in 2009. It encompasses all the rights and freedoms contained in the **ECHR**. It also adds all the rights found in the case law of the Court of Justice of the European Union (CJEU). This book is about rights under the **ECHR** but there is an overlap, e.g., the right to respect for a private and family life under **Article 8** of the **ECHR** is in the **EU Charter** but there it is **Article 7**.

Task 3

We saw that the law is only involved when someone breaks legal rules, not social ones. Social rules may be enforced by society's disapproval of any breach of the rules. Legal rules are enforced by a formal body set up for this purpose, e.g., a court or tribunal.

Imagine you are with a group of people stranded on a desert island. You need to make some rules to govern behaviour. Make a list of three rules you think are important and two rights you think should be protected. Now go on to decide if they should have the force of law and how they will be enforced.

Self-test questions

1. Liability is based on individual responsibility. What is the main difference between criminal and civil responsibility?
2. What is the main difference between a claim and a right freedom?
3. What did Lord Scarman say in Kwawaja?
4. What is the arbitrary use of power?

Chapter 2 A brief history of the development of human rights in Europe

Human rights in international law

Although certain rights have been around for centuries, when looking at the background to the present situation it is sensible to start with the period following World War Two.

The Second World War and its aftermath

After World War Two, England, France and Germany recognised a need for cooperation instead of adversity. In a speech in Zurich in 1946, Winston Churchill suggested that France and Germany should form a partnership and referred to a *"kind of United States of Europe"*. This could arguably be said to be the starting point for both the European Union and the European Convention on Human Rights. Although some years passed before the European Union (as it is now called) was created, the idea of European human rights began to emerge soon after this speech.

The United Nations and the Universal Declaration of Human Rights 1948

The **European Convention on Human Rights** (**ECHR**) is formally called the Convention for the Protection of Human Rights and Fundamental Freedoms. It was introduced by the Council of Europe to give effect to the Universal Declaration of Human Rights. This had been proclaimed by the United Nations in 1948 but lacked enforcement mechanisms. The Convention was opened for signature in Rome on 4 November 1950 and came into force in 1953. It included many of the rights in the Universal Declaration of Human Rights and is binding on all signatories, known as 'States Parties' (more commonly just called states).

The Council of Europe should not be confused with the European Union (EU) institutions; it is a separate body, formed in 1949 by the Treaty of London to uphold democracy, human rights and the rule of law. However, as it says on its website, the Council of Europe works in close partnership with the EU. It also co-operates with the United Nations, the Organization for Security and Co-operation in Europe, and with partner countries in its neighbourhood and worldwide. All EU member states are signatories to the **ECHR** and thus members of the Council of Europe.

The Council of Europe and the ECHR

The **ECHR** was first signed by ten countries, the United Kingdom, France, Ireland, Belgium, Denmark, Italy, Luxembourg, the Netherlands, Norway and Sweden. The aim of the Council of Europe at the time was the achievement of greater unity between its members and the Convention was intended to help accomplish this. According to the website of the Council of Europe, the governments which signed the declaration had *"a common heritage of political traditions, ideals, freedom and the rule of law"*.

There are now 47 members making up the Council of Europe. The Council of Europe has a Committee of Ministers to make decisions on policy and a Parliament to provide a forum for debate and to elect the judges for the European Court of Human Rights (ECtHR).

The ECtHR is a permanent court set up to guarantee the rights protected by the **ECHR**. Judges are elected by the Committee from across the participating states but are supposed to be independent of their own countries when passing judgment. The court is open to states and individuals regardless of nationality. There is more on this in Chapter 6 on the enforcement of rights.

Although the formal name uses the term *"fundamental freedoms"* the rights given under the **ECHR** are fundamental rights. Each *"freedom"* is a right to that freedom, thus in **Article 10** what is commonly referred to as freedom of expression is actually the right to freedom of expression. This type of right is what Hohfeld called a *"claim-right"* as discussed in the previous chapter. This is because the **ECHR** gives the rights and imposes a corresponding duty on the state to guarantee them.

Since 1950 the **ECHR** has been amended several times and various protocols have added new rights. The UK has only signed up to a few of these extra rights. These are the first three Articles in **Protocol 1** (protection of property, the right to education and the right to free elections) and **Protocol 13** which abolished the death penalty across all states. The original **ECHR** set out 13 rights. Under **Article 1** the signatories to the **ECHR** agreed to secure to everyone within their jurisdiction the rights and freedoms defined in the Convention. These rights were contained in **Articles 2** to **14**. **Article 15** allows for derogations from these rights (except the right to life) in time of emergency. Here is an overview of the Articles needed for OCR and Eduqas A level.

Article	Brief explanation	More detail
Article 5	Right to liberty and security of person	No one shall be deprived of his liberty save in the following cases and in accordance with a procedure prescribed by law Various methods of arrest and detention are then listed **A 5 (3)** requires that anyone arrested or detained as allowed above must be brought promptly before a judge or other officer authorised by law
Article 6	Right to a fair trial	In the determination of his civil rights and obligations or of any criminal charge against him, everyone is entitled to a fair and public hearing within a reasonable time by an independent and impartial tribunal established by law
Article 8	Right to respect for a private and family life	Everyone has the right to respect for his private and family life, his home and his correspondence
Article 10	Right to freedom of expression	Everyone has the right to freedom of expression. This right shall include the freedom to hold opinions and to receive and impart information and ideas without interference by public authority and regardless of frontiers
Article 11	Right to freedom of assembly and association	Everyone has the right to freedom of peaceful assembly and to freedom of association with others, including the right to form and to join trade unions for the protection of his interests

The **ECHR** imposes both negative and positive obligations on all participating states. The state has a negative duty not to interfere with the rights and a positive duty to take action to protect them. The rights have different values in that some are absolute and some are either limited or qualified.

There are times when a state may avoid its obligations, this is known as derogation. Derogation from all articles (except **A 2** the right to life) is allowed under **A 15** in time of *"war or other public emergency threatening the life of the nation"* and to the extent derogation is *"strictly required"* by the situation. **A 15** does not apply to **A 2**, except to deaths resulting from lawful acts of war. The only other exceptions are following a sentence of a court on conviction of a crime for which this penalty is provided by law or in self-defence. The death penalty was abolished in England in 1965. It was abolished by the **ECHR** in most circumstances in 1983 and in all circumstances including times of war in 2002 under **Protocol 13**. Protocols are not compulsory; they only apply to those who have chosen to sign up to them.

In addition to derogation, the state is allowed a margin of appreciation in how to interpret and apply **ECHR** rights. This means neither the positive nor the negative obligation is absolute, it allows for discretion. The state has discretion when deciding on how far it must protect the right (the positive obligation) and interference may be justified where it is *"necessary in a democratic society"* (the negative obligation). The term *"margin of appreciation"* was first used to describe the use of the derogation powers under **A 15** but has been used by the ECtHR in many other cases. In 2013 it was formally introduced into the **ECHR**. On signing, all parties to the **ECHR** agreed to secure the rights and freedoms included in it for their citizens. **Protocol 15** adds *"that in doing so they enjoy a margin of appreciation"* to the introduction to the **ECHR**. There is a proviso that this is subject to the supervisory jurisdiction of the ECtHR.

The margin of appreciation applies to all rights but is widest in the three qualified rights under **Articles 8**, **10** and **11**. This and the grounds on which interference may be justified are discussed in Chapter 4.

Task 4

Briefly explain what derogation means and the limits to it.

Human rights in the UK before the Human Rights Act 1998 (HRA)

The **ECHR** was binding on all signatories from the time of signing. That means the UK has had an international obligation to protect human rights since 1950. There are also many domestic laws which protect rights.

The right to life is a principle in most democratic states and underpins the natural law view of justice. This is protected in the UK by laws against killing and by the removal of capital punishment. This is equivalent to the right under **A 2** of the **ECHR**. Although there is no written constitution providing for human rights in the UK, even before the **HRA** many freedoms and some rights existed. The right to liberty (**A 5**) is arguably one of the earliest examples of human rights. The English equivalent is the doctrine of *habeas corpus* which was introduced during the 12th century. The Latin translates as *"that you have the body"*. It means that a person who has been detained by the state or another body can apply for a writ of *habeas corpus* to challenge that detention. The writ would order that the person must be brought before a court of law to decide whether the detention was lawful.

Magna Carta, the Bill of Rights and the rule of law

The doctrine of *habeas corpus* was included in the Magna Carta in 1215. This is the first formal declaration of the right to liberty, now contained in **Article 5** of the **ECHR**. It is also seen in **A 6** as the doctrine ensures people are brought before a court of law. The Magna Carta formally guaranteed the doctrine of *habeas corpus* introduced the previous century. It also restricted the power of the king and increased the power of the people. It is still an important right in

England today, even though the rights to liberty and a fair trial are now included in the **ECHR**. In **R v Secretary of State for the Home Department Ex parte Kwawaja 1984**, Lord Scarman said that case law had made clear that *habeas corpus* protection is not limited to British nationals. It should apply to anyone subject to English law because those who are subject to the law should also be entitled to its protection. That the law should apply equally to all is one of Lord Bingham's sub-rules to the rule of law discussed in the previous chapter.

The **Bill of Rights 1689** was enacted after the English civil wars and further limited the power of the monarch (Charles II). It put certain freedoms into statutory form, such as freedom from *"cruel and unusual punishment"* which formed the basis for an amendment to the American constitution and for the **Universal Declaration of Human Rights**. The latter prohibited *"cruel, inhuman or degrading treatment or punishment"* and this formed the basis for **Article 3** of the **ECHR**.

Freedom of the person is seen in early theories of justice especially those of libertarians like John Mill. As we noted in the previous chapter, English law is based on residual freedoms rather than rights. This means that a person is free to act unless prohibited from doing so by law. The concept of parliamentary sovereignty as developed in English law further enhances such freedoms as it provides that no-one, not even the monarch, is above Parliament (an essential part of the rule of law). Thus, no king or queen can restrict a citizen's freedom unless authorised by an Act of Parliament. Scotland produced an equivalent to the Bill of rights but neither applied in Northern Ireland. The constitutional effect of the **HRA** is discussed further under Human Rights in the UK after the **HRA 1998**.

The freedom to meet with others and to protest has long been a tradition in English law. In **Beatty v Gillbanks 1882**, the court ruled that people had the right to march peacefully and lawfully even though another group opposed them and thus threaten trouble. Although there are many restrictions on this right, mainly in public order legislation, it is similar to the right to freedom of assembly provided by **A 11**.

There is no privacy law as such in the UK but the tort of breach of confidence protects information given in confidence. Traditionally this required a relationship of confidence between the parties (a duty of confidentiality) but this has been relaxed since the **HRA** and the tort of misuse of private information has developed. This is nearer to the right to respect for a private life under **A 8**.

Freedom of the press to report in criticism of the state and for people to talk freely and openly about problems with the government has also long been a tradition in the UK and this is similar to **A 10**.

All these are residual freedoms and so allowed, subject to any law prohibiting them.

The rule of law, discussed in Chapter 1 developed alongside the **Bill of Rights** and parliamentary sovereignty. The preamble to the **Universal Declaration of Human Rights** says that if people are not to be compelled to rebel against tyranny and oppression that *"human rights should be protected by the rule of law"*.

These were all important principles for UK citizens because although the UK had signed the **ECHR** in 1953, it had not brought it into domestic law. They are still important as it is under domestic laws that all cases claiming human rights start.

Task 5

Choose two articles and explain how UK citizens may have had similar protection before the UK signed the **ECHR**.

Status of the ECHR in the UK and the impact of decisions of the ECtHR

As the **ECHR** was not part of domestic law, people who wanted to enforce their rights had to take the matter up in Europe by way of a petition to the European Commission of Human Rights. Challenges to the state or others who had violated a person's rights could be made by UK citizens only in their domestic courts until 1966. Although a state could bring a case against another state, the right for individuals to petition was not compulsory under the **ECHR**.

Even after 1966, individuals first had to exhaust domestic procedures and remedies and then petition the European Commission of Human Rights which would investigate the matter. If no agreement could be reached the case would go to the ECtHR. The Commission decided on the admissibility of a complaint and then the Committee and/or Court determined the merits of cases which came before them to decide whether there had been a violation or not.

 Few individuals had the time and money to go through this process and even if they did, decisions of the ECtHR had no binding force in the UK. An example is **Malone v Commissioner of Police for the Metropolis 1979** where the domestic court refused to rule that measures which allowed the interception of telephone communications breached **Article 8** (the right to respect for a private and family life). When the case went to Strasbourg, in **Malone v UK 1984**, the ECtHR ruled that the English measures breached **A 8**. The government responded by passing another law explicitly allowing telephone tapping. The impact of the ECtHR judgment in this case was non-existent. In fact the result made the law worse in that interception was now allowed by an Act of Parliament. State surveillance may be needed in the interests of public safety but can be intrusive. It is cases like this where the **HRA** may help (see next section)

Malone can also be used to illustrate the time it can take for a case to get to the ECtHR. The problem was that there was no right to petition the court without first exhausting domestic remedies (as is still the case). In the UK, even the right to petition was not given to individuals until 1966. It was not mandatory and the UK had opted out. Challenging an interference with rights was therefore a lengthy, costly and complex process. The **HRA** was designed to deal with this situation and allow the British people to seek redress within their own courts instead of in Europe. However, in practice the effect of using the national courts was and is limited because the courts cannot provide a remedy if the interference is allowed within national law or where there is a clear conflict between the domestic law and the **ECHR**.

Case example

Kaye v Robertson 1990 involved the actor who played the lead role of René in "Hello, Hello" on television. He had been seriously injured in an accident. While lying in bed in hospital following brain surgery, a journalist sneaked in and tried to interview him. He took several photographs without permission and the family wanted to prevent publication. Despite stating that the journalist had been grossly irresponsible and had invaded the actor's privacy, the CA held that this was not against the UK law. The case led to severe criticism of the law and there was a public campaign for greater protection of privacy. The CA itself said the case was a *"graphic illustration"* of the need for Parliament to act to protect privacy. It has not done so but cases after the **HRA** (see below) have met with greater success.

Although not enforceable prior to the **HRA** (and not strictly enforceable after it), Convention rights were often secured by UK citizens because the UK Government did not want to be seen to be going against rulings of the ECtHR.

Examples of where the law was changed following a ruling of the ECtHR include:

Case	Brief facts	Article breached by UK	Changes made
Golder v UK 1973	A prisoner was refused access to a solicitor	The prisoner's right to a fair trial **A 6**	An increase in prisoners" rights leading to **PACE 1984**
Sunday Times v UK 1979	The government used laws on contempt of court to prohibit the Times from publishing information about a drug which caused birth defects	The newspaper's right to freedom of expression **A 10**	The **Contempt of Court Act 1981** amended the law on contempt
Campbell and Cosans 1982	A mother challenged a school's use of corporal punishment	A child's right to freedom from torture or inhuman or degrading treatment or punishment **A 3**	Corporal punishment was banned in most schools
Benham v UK 1996	A man was imprisoned for non-payment of the poll tax without being allowed legal aid and representation	The prisoner's right to liberty (**A 5**) was not breached as imprisonment followed a court case The right to a fair trial (**A 6**) was breached as he had a right to representation	The rights to a duty solicitor for free advice and representation were strengthened
Thompson and Venables 1999	Children were tried in an adult court under adult procedures	The prisoners' right to a fair trial **A 6**	Special procedures were established for youth trials

The system for bringing a case changed in 1998 when **Protocol 11**, concerning the right to petition (added to the **ECHR** in 1994) came into force. The **HRA** was passed in the same year and came into effect two years later.

Summary of the development of human rights

1948	The Universal Declaration of Human Rights was proclaimed by the United Nations
1949	The Council of Europe was formed by the Treaty of London
1950	The European Convention on Human Rights (ECHR) was opened for signature in Rome
1953	The ECHR came into force
1966	The right to petition the ECtHR (*via* the Commission) was introduced in the UK
1994	Protocol 11 was added to the ECHR making the right to petition compulsory and direct to the court
1998	Protocol 11 came into force
1998	The Human Rights Act (HRA) was passed
2000	The HRA came into force

Human rights in the UK after the Human Rights Act 1998

Although the UK was an early signatory to the **ECHR**, the rights agreed upon did not become part of UK law until the **Human Rights Act 1998** (**HRA**) came into force in 2000. The **HRA** effectively brings the rights into UK law so if human rights have been breached, individuals affected can take their case to a national court rather than having to seek justice "*in Europe*" from the ECtHR. This demonstrates a movement from residual freedoms to claim rights.

The **HRA** was introduced by the Labour government in 1996 but took a long time to go through Parliament. Here is the time-table:

December 1996	• Green Paper
October 1997	• White Paper called 'Rights Brought Home' October 1997 published, detailing main provisions
October 1997	• Draft Bill published • First Reading in the House of Lords
November 1997	• Second Reading
February 1998	• Committee Stage and Report Stage • Third Reading in the Lords
Feb to May 1998	• To the other house, the Commons • First Reading and Second Reading
May 1998	• Committee Stage in the Commons • Report Stage and Third Reading
November 1998	• Royal Assent
October 2000	• Became law

Incorporation and interpretation of the ECHR

Although the Convention rights are not directly incorporated into the law of the UK, the **HRA** does have that effect up to a point. Several sections of the **HRA** are directed at the legislature and the national courts and tribunals and these aim to secure **ECHR** rights for UK citizens. You should learn the main ones.

S 2 of the **HRA** requires judges to take account of decisions of the ECtHR.

S 3 states that *"so far as it is possible to do so, primary legislation and subordinate legislation must be read and given effect in a way which is compatible with the Convention rights"*.

Under **s 4** if the court is satisfied that the provision is incompatible with a Convention right, it may make a declaration of that incompatibility. However, **s 4 (6)** adds that a declaration of incompatibility *"does not affect the validity, continuing operation or enforcement of the provision in respect of which it is given; and is not binding on the parties to the proceedings in which it is made"*.

S 2 and **s 3** taken together effectively involve judges indirectly incorporating the rights contained in the **ECHR** by way of interpretation, either of decisions of the ECtHR or of the **ECHR** articles. However, **s 4(6)** makes clear that judges cannot affect the validity of the law. This means that a judge cannot set aside a law that conflicts with the **ECHR**, only issue a declaration that the law is not compatible. It is then up to the state to decide whether to amend the law to comply with the **ECHR**. Although once a declaration is made the state will usually amend the law accordingly, it did so before the **HRA** (see table of examples prior to the **HRA**). The fact is that it does not have to even after the passing of the **HRA**. The effect is that there may be no remedy for an individual whose rights have been violated.

Case example

In **Hirst v UK 2005** a blanket ban on allowing prisoners to vote was declared incompatible with **A 8** of the **ECHR**. The UK did not amend the law to comply with the **ECHR**.

S 6 makes it unlawful for public authorities to act in a way that is incompatible with the **ECHR**. This includes not only courts and tribunals, but also anyone whose functions are of a public nature (police, local authorities, hospitals and state schools) to respect and protect human rights. However, it does not include either House of Parliament or a person exercising functions in connection with proceedings in Parliament.

S 7 provides that a person can bring a claim in the domestic courts where a public authority acts in violation of **s 6**. However, there is a proviso that this can only be done by someone who is a *"victim of the unlawful act"*. This means only those directly affected by a breach of the right can challenge the legality of the breach.

The effect of **s 6** and **s 7** taken together is to create a statutory tort whereby individuals affected can enforce **ECHR** rights against public authorities for non-compliance. However, **s 8** provides that the court may only award compensation (damages) where it is satisfied that the award is necessary to afford just satisfaction to the claimant. (Just satisfaction comes under **A 41** of the **ECHR** and is discussed under enforcement in Chapter 6.)

Case example

Commissioner of Police of the Metropolis v DSD and another 2018 followed the arrest of the London taxi driver Worboys for a number of serious attacks. Several victims brought claims against the police under **s 7** for failure to conduct effective investigations into his crimes. They alleged that this was not a general duty owed to the public at large but a specific one to investigate crimes which cause serious harm to an individual. The claims relied on **A 3** against torture which you don't need, but illustrate **s 6** and **s 7 HRA** as well as taking account of ECtHR decisions (**s 2**). The SC held that obligations under the **ECHR** had a different basis of liability so could not be compared to the duty of care in tort. The protective duty under the **ECHR** did not depend on whether it was fair, just and reasonable. In addition, the court is a public authority so has to comply with **s 6** and act compatibly with the **ECHR** when reaching a decision. It must also take account of ECtHR decisions under **s 2**. In conclusion, there was a breach of the duty to investigate.

So, **s 7 HRA** provides for the rights under the **ECHR** to have direct effect between an individual and a public authority, i.e., vertical direct effect. It does not provide for rights to have direct effect between individuals, i.e., no horizontal direct effect. However, horizontal indirect effect may be possible *via* **s 3** which requires that the national law must be interpreted to comply where possible. The court is also a public authority under **s 6** so must itself comply with the **ECHR**. This will further strengthen the requirement to ensure domestic law complies. The courts have developed various domestic laws by way of the **HRA** such as the tort of misuse of private information which developed from the older tort of breach of confidence. This is an example of how **s 3** can give horizontal direct effect. However, there must be a national law to interpret.

S 19 provides that every bill put before Parliament must contain a statement saying that it is compatible with the **ECHR** or that it is not and this was intended. This means that Parliament will usually make sure that new laws are compatible with **ECHR** rights and under **s 2** and **3** the courts will, where possible, interpret laws in a way which is compatible with these rights.

The overall effect of all these sections is that Parliament can pass conflicting laws but must take the **HRA** into account (**s 19**). When a person takes the case to a domestic court (**s 7**), judges must take account of decisions of the **ECtHR** (**s 2**) and if domestic law cannot be interpreted to comply (**s 3**) the courts can make a declaration of incompatibility (**s 4**). If the claim is against a public authority it can be in reliance on **s 7 HRA**.

The **HRA** applies to most articles. Exceptions are **A 1** (the agreement to secure all ECHR rights) and **A 13** (the right to an effective remedy). These are not covered by the provisions in the **HRA**, mainly because the UK felt that by passing the **HRA** it had both secured the rights and provided an effective remedy within domestic law. This does not mean the UK has no obligation under these articles. As a signatory to the **ECHR** it has an international obligation. However, it does not have a domestic one.

The introduction of the **HRA** supports the rights of individuals and offers greater protection to those whose rights have been violated. These are often people coming from minority groups who have little chance of making their voice heard. Transsexuals, prisoners and mental health patients have used the **HRA** and/or the **ECHR** to safeguard their rights. Most have relied on **A 8** which protects the right to a private and family life and case examples are given in Chapter 4. Others have relied on the prohibition of discrimination in **A 14**. This is not on the specifications but you will see references to it in cases because it is often relied on with, or as an alternative to, other rights.

Morals and justice: The protection of human rights accords with natural law as it is based on moral values. It also accords with the libertarian view in the cases of certain rights, e.g., those which support personal autonomy. Although it appears to be against the utilitarian theory of justice, it can be said that society itself benefits from certain rights being enshrined in law and so protection of rights increases the greater good.

Example

Anti-terrorism laws are arguably for the greater good of society. At one time, suspects could be held indefinitely without being charged. A utilitarian could argue that the ends justify the means. An alternative argument would be that society itself is weakened by going against the rule of law. These laws could be seen as against "natural" law as they conflict with the concept that no-one should be imprisoned without a fair trial. This is also against the rule of law.

When they signed the **ECHR**, all states undertook to abide by the final judgment of the ECtHR in any case to which they were parties. For the UK, this means that even if the **HRA** was repealed it would still have an international obligation to uphold and protect rights until and unless it withdrew from the **ECHR**.

There is a parliamentary Joint Committee on Human Rights which scrutinises government measures for their compatibility with the **ECHR**. It also monitors the Government's response to judgments on human rights from the ECtHR and UK courts.

The main advantage of the **HRA** is that it allows people to rely on the **ECHR** in the national courts. Although it is still the case that domestic remedies must be exhausted before a petition can be made to the ECtHR, it is more likely that a domestic remedy *will* be available. Even though the courts cannot overturn an Act of Parliament, a decision that the law is incompatible may have a political effect. Governments may react and change the law rather than be seen to be abusing human rights. As the SC points out on its website *"Although a declaration of incompatibility does not place any legal obligation on the government to amend or repeal legislation, it sends a clear message to legislators that they should change the law to make it compatible with the human rights set out in the Convention"*.

Evaluation pointer

A declaration under **s 4** may send a clear message but the government may not listen. An example is **Hirst**. In addition, despite **s 2** there have been times when the domestic courts have not followed the ECtHR. An example is **Horncastle 2009**, discussed below. This reduces the effectiveness of human rights law. On the plus side, although we saw that changes to the law also happened before the **HRA**, the person affected had to take the case to Strasbourg if the domestic courts did not provide a remedy. Now that remedy can be more easily achieved at home. A second positive point to make about **s 4** is that it has the effect of remitting the issue to Parliament where there can be a proper debate. The result will be a political decision informed by the court's view of the law. That seems to be an appropriate way to consider changes to the law, with the law-makers in partnership.

Task 6

Briefly explain how **sections 2, 3** and **4** of the **HRA** affect human rights.

In addition to the **HRA** *"bringing rights home"* in 2000, the system for bringing a case changed when **Protocol 11** came into force in 1998. **Protocol 11** establishes a single, full-time Court to replace the Commission and ECtHR. Unlike other protocols added over the years this is not optional and all states had to ratify it before it came into force. The Protocol makes the right of individual petition and the jurisdiction of the court compulsory and indefinite for participating States. Previously, states could allow individual petitions or not, and although the UK had allowed this since 1966 it was on a temporary basis renewed every five years. The situation now is that the citizens of all states that have signed the **ECHR** have the right to petition the court directly. This should reduce costs and speed things up, although the person claiming violation of a right must still go through the domestic courts before petitioning the ECtHR. This seems a waste of time. However, since the **HRA** it should mean that the national court protects the right by way of **s 2** or **3** so that there is no need to go to the ECtHR. A court is also a public authority so has an obligation to protect rights under **s 6**.

Summary of the effect of the HRA

S 2 & 3	means the courts should interpret in line with both the ECtHR and the ECHR
S 4	allows a declaration of incompatibility to be made where this is not possible
S 6 & 7	effectively create a tort of failure to comply enforceable by individuals against public authorities

If a petition is made to the ECtHR it may go before a single judge, a committee of three judges or a chamber of seven judges. The court will establish whether the case is admissible. As before, it will attempt to reach a friendly settlement but this will be done by the court not the Commission or Committee. If no settlement is reached the court (the chamber) will pass judgment or refer the case to a grand chamber of seventeen judges. The role of the Committee under the new procedure is to supervise the execution of the judgment. The final step will be the payment of compensation by the state and/or amendment of the law to comply with the **ECHR**.

Task 7

Give three case examples of where the law was changed following a ruling of the ECtHR even before the **HRA** came into force.

Impact of decisions of the ECtHR on the UK

A common mistake is to refer to the ECtHR as an appeal court. The effect is similar, but although individuals must attempt to achieve a domestic remedy first, the case is a *petition to* the ECtHR claiming a right under the **ECHR**, not an *appeal from* a domestic court based on national law. Judges in the UK must abide by **s 2** of the **HRA** and take account of ECtHR judgments as well as interpret UK law in line with the **ECHR** in so far as it is possible to do so under **s 3**.

The difference is that although individuals must attempt to achieve a domestic remedy first, if there is no remedy in the national courts the claimant will make a petition to the ECtHR based on the **ECHR** provisions, not an appeal based on national law.

Evaluation pointer

Note the "take account of" and "in so far as it is possible". Neither section is absolute which lessens the impact somewhat.

Judges in the ECtHR tend to be quite libertarian in nature and they use a purposive approach to interpretation. This has had some effect on English judges and there has been movement away from the conservative tendency shown in the past. Independence of the judiciary is part of the rule of law and **A 10** provides for freedom of expression to be curtailed *"for maintaining the authority and impartiality of the judiciary"*. A judiciary free from political bias is particularly important in human rights law where it is usually the state that is being challenged.

A further effect is that the ECtHR sees the **ECHR** as a living instrument. This means the law should develop and evolve with changing circumstances such as technological advances and changing social values. An example is the development of the right under **A 8** to encompass same-sex couples and transsexuals. Judges in both the ECtHR and domestic courts are encouraged actively to pursue the enhancement of human rights. Cases like this illustrate the link between human rights and law and technology.

On its website the SC refers to the requirement in **s 2** to take account of decisions of the ECtHR and adds a quote from Lord Bingham that no national court should *"without strong reason dilute or weaken the effect of the Strasbourg case law"*. This suggests that, even in cases of conflict, the courts will attempt to follow ECtHR judgments and protect rights if that is at all possible.

Decisions of the ECtHR impact on constitutional arrangements in the UK as well as the law. Under **s 2 HRA** ECtHR decisions must be taken into account by the domestic courts. The devolutionary settlements with Scotland, Northern Ireland and Wales all included the **HRA** and Convention rights and any attempt at repeal of the **HRA** could damage these devolution arrangements (England is considering replacing it with a Bill of Rights, see Chapter 7). In addition, the Good Friday agreement in Northern Ireland was based on incorporation of the **ECHR**. As the **HRA** is entrenched in these legislatures and constrains their ability to legislate, repeal of the **HRA** is likely to require their consent. A convention (called the Sewel convention) was established in 1998 when power was devolved to Scotland and this provides that the UK Parliament will not normally legislate on devolved matters without consent. This has since been expanded to require consent for others matters which could affect the powers of the devolved parliaments. The Scottish First Minister has already said that Scotland would not consent. Any attempt at repeal without consent could cause a constitutional crisis.

The main impact of decisions of the ECtHR is on parliamentary sovereignty, or at least it appears to be. Many argue that decisions of European judges are affecting UK laws. This is only partly true because although a government *may* change the law to comply with a judgment of the ECtHR it does not *have* to, as seen in **Hirst**. Another impact is on the power of the executive, as human rights cases are generally challenging the state or public authority (unlike the **ECHR**, the **HRA** only applies to public authorities not individuals). Although usually exercising powers given by Parliament, ministers and local authorities are using delegated legislation which has limited parliamentary scrutiny. That is why such measures are subject to judicial review and if they are challenged, the court will have to take account of ECtHR decisions when making a judgment.

A final point on the impact of decisions of the ECtHR is that there may not be one, or rather the impact may work both ways. It has been known for the ECtHR to follow the UK Supreme Court.

Example

In **Horncastle 2009** the SC declined to follow a decision of the ECtHR in **Al-Khawaja 2009**. The effect was that when the latter case went back to the ECtHR in **Al-Khawaja 2011** the SC decision was followed. On its website the SC noted that these cases had been perceived as demonstrating the concept of a dialogue between the two courts.

Summary of the effect of the HRA and ECHR

A claim may be based on domestic law or it may be based directly on the **ECHR** right.

Bringing a claim for breach of a right

What it the claim?	What is the law?	The role of the ECtHR?
A claim based on domestic law in a domestic court	Use the relevant domestic law e.g., contempt of court Support the claim by way of **s 2** and **s 3 HRA** The claim can be against a public authority or individual Judicial review of the measure is an alternative against a public authority	If the claim and any appeals fail petition the ECtHR If the claim is admissible the court will rule as to whether the state has met its obligations under the **ECHR** If not the claim will succeed and the Commission will order the state to provide just satisfaction
A claim based on the **ECHR** in a domestic court	Use **s 7 HRA** Support the claim by way of **s 2** and **s 3 HRA** The claim can only be against a public authority Judicial review is an alternative	
A claim based on the **ECHR** in the ECtHR	Use the **ECHR** but only if domestic laws have been exhausted	

One thing to note is that although many of the cases on human rights are claims to the right, the **ECHR** and **HRA** can also be used in defending a civil claim or a prosecution.

Criticisms and reform of human rights – see Chapter 7

It is easier to evaluate the topic after looking at some specific rights.

Self-test questions

1. What must you do before going to the ECtHR to claim a right?
2. What was the aim of the Council of Europe when it introduced the ECHR?
3. What does s 19 HRA provide?
4. What does Protocol 11 provide and is it optional?

5. *What is parliamentary sovereignty and how is it affected by decisions of the ECtHR?*

Chapter 3 Rights and restrictions under Articles 5 and 6 of the ECHR

Now we have seen the effect of the **HRA** we can consider the individual rights it aims to protect. Many of the rights and freedoms given under the **ECHR** overlap with others. You will therefore see some of the rights discussed under more than one section. I have put the cases under the right that appears most dominant. **A 5** and **A 6** are limited rights with only a few exceptions, this chapter therefore covers the rights, restrictions and provisions of English law together.

Most rights have limitations or restrictions. This means that rights may be sacrificed in the interests of, e.g., state security or public health. In this case individual rights are subordinated to the public interest. Thus the right to liberty and the right to a fair hearing under **A 5** and **A 6** can be restricted by anti-terrorism laws in the interests of security, discussed below.

As we saw earlier, **A 15** also allows for derogation from the **ECHR** in time of *"war or other public emergency threatening the life of the nation"*.

Examination pointer

The best way to understand how the rights apply in practice is by looking at cases brought claiming those rights in different situations. I have therefore used a range of cases to illustrate. You don't need to learn them all but should have at least one for each article where the right was upheld and one where it was denied. This will help you answer an application question where you are not sure if the right will be upheld or not.

The right to liberty under Article 5

Article 5 (1) provides that:

Everyone has the right to liberty and security of person. No one shall be deprived of his liberty save in the following cases and in accordance with a procedure prescribed by law

There is a negative obligation on the state not to interfere in a person's liberty. This means keeping state activities which restrict liberties to a minimum. There is a positive obligation to protect a person's liberty. This means having laws prohibiting acts that restrict it and extends to regulating activities of individuals which restrict the liberty of other individuals, e.g., by having laws against false imprisonment, human trafficking and kidnapping. The state should also provide for investigative procedures and remedies where a loss of liberty has occurred. The right includes 'security of person' which means there is some overlap with **A 2**.

A 5 is a limited right and includes specific exceptions. These exceptions mainly concern police powers of arrest, detention and stop and search, all of which restrict liberty and are discussed below under restrictions. Other less obvious restrictions include forced hospital care, detention in schools and even the subsidiary elements of detention in respect of prison sentences. These are unlikely to be the focus of an examination question. Where I have used such cases it is to help you to see what amounts to a deprivation of liberty. This is important as if there is no deprivation of liberty, there will be no claim.

What is deprivation of liberty?

The ECtHR guide to **A 5** differentiates between restrictions on movement serious enough to come within **A 5** and mere restrictions of liberty. It makes clear the distinction is one of degree or intensity, and not one of nature or substance. Relevant matters include the type, duration, effects and manner of implementation of the measure in question. The guide also states that the purpose of the measures taken is not decisive for the assessment of whether there has been a deprivation of liberty. The court only takes this into account later, when deciding if the deprivation is compatible with **A 5**.

Here are three case examples involving the UK. The first example went to the HL and then the ECtHR and the second shows the SC interpretation of the distinction. The third is a further example from the ECtHR.

Case examples

In **v Commissioner of Police for the Metropolis 2009**, the HL accepted the government's argument that the police confining people in Oxford Circus during demonstrations for seven hours was not a deprivation of liberty. The HL noted that the difference between deprivation of and restriction upon liberty is one of degree and whether it amounts to violation of the right to liberty under **A 5** will depend on the circumstances. The application of **A 5** to *"kettling"* as a method of crowd control had not yet been the subject of a case in the ECtHR. In **Austin v UK 2012**, the ECtHR noted that the **ECHR** was a living instrument and should be read in light of modern conditions. The court agreed with the HL that the circumstances were relevant and that in deciding whether there had been a deprivation of liberty account must be taken of a *"whole range of criteria such as the type, duration, effects and manner of implementation of the measure in question"*. The ECtHR concluded that there was no deprivation of liberty but made clear that the fact that the measure was necessary to prevent serious injury or damage was relevant. Had it not been then the 'type' of measure would have been different and its coercive nature could have engaged **A 5**.

Both the HL and the ECtHR referred to the *"paradigm"* situation of confinement in a prison cell where there would no argument that there was a deprivation of liberty. Both agreed that in other cases the difference between a restriction upon liberty and deprivation of liberty is one of degree and that the circumstances needed careful examination.

In **Cheshire West and Chester Council v P 2014**, the SC ruled that people who had been placed in care by the council against their wishes had been deprived of their right to liberty under **A 5** and that the right also applied to those without capacity to make their own decisions. The SC held that the *"acid test"* for deprivation of liberty is whether the person is under continuous supervision and control and is not free to leave. If so this is deprivation of liberty not a mere restriction on liberty. Whether or not the person was compliant was not relevant. Any deprivation of liberty had to be necessary and in the person's best interest. The council had violated **A 5** because there were no proper safeguards or checks to ensure this was the case.

In **James v UK 2012**, the ECtHR held that denying access to rehabilitation courses to prisoners serving indeterminate public protection (IPP) sentences breached **A 5**. These sentences are made up of the tariff followed by an indefinite period which continues until such time as a Parole Board finds there is no longer a risk to the public. The ECtHR held that once the punishment part of an IPP sentence had been served there should be a real opportunity for rehabilitation. The delays and lack of access meant there was no chance of going through the prison system – and coming out of it – because the Parole Board required evidence of rehabilitation before release. This violated the right to liberty as prisoners may be kept in detention longer than would be the case with rehabilitation.

The ECtHR guide notes that there is both a subjective element (the person has not validly consented to the confinement) and an objective element (confinement is in a particular restricted space for a not negligible length of time). The next two cases illustrate these.

Consent may be relevant but not conclusive. In **Storck v. Germany 2005**, the ECtHR held that the fact that the claimant had consented to her stay in a psychiatric clinic did not prevent it being a deprivation of liberty contrary to **A 5**. This is similar to **Cheshire West** above. However, in this case it was not the state which had confined her but private medical practitioners. The ECtHR held that Germany had violated its positive obligation to protect her against interference with her liberty under **A 5** by not ensuring *"competent and regular supervisory control against a deprivation of liberty"*. Another point of relevance was that she had escaped and this showed lack of consent to any continued detention even if she had consented in the first place. In addition, the state had some involvement, as it was the police who returned her to the clinic.

In **Guzzardi v Italy 1980**, the ECtHR looked again at the relevant objective factors. A man had been confined to an island because he was suspected of being involved in criminal activities. The ECtHR held that being confined to an island was sufficient to be a deprivation of liberty. The court attached particular significance to the extremely small size of the area where he was confined, the almost permanent supervision to which he was subject, the all but complete impossibility for him to make social contacts and the length of his enforced stay. The court likened the situation to an open prison.

The paradigm example of deprivation of liberty is being detained in a police cell or similar involuntary enforced custody. This will almost certainly be a deprivation of liberty even if the detention is relatively short. Then the court will need to decide if the deprivation violates **A 5** or is justified in the circumstances.

Case examples

In **Murray v the UK 1996**, being held in custody at an army centre for less than three hours for questioning was sufficient to engage **A 5**.

Ostendorf v Germany 2013 involved the detention in Germany before an international football match of a person who was a known football hooligan. He was held for about four hours and released when the match was over. The ECtHR held that **A 5** protects the physical liberty of the person and is not concerned with mere restrictions upon liberty of movement. However, it added that *"having regard to its case-law"* he had been deprived of his liberty. The court noted that *"Convention institutions have repeatedly found"* that being brought to a police station against one's will and being held in a cell amounted to a deprivation of liberty, even if the interference lasted for a relatively short duration. However, on the facts it did not breach **A 5**.

In some cases the length of detention may mean **A 5** is not engaged as in **Austin**. **Austin** which suggests that there is a threshold to be crossed before **A 5** is engaged and that this must be measured by the degree or intensity of the restriction. Thus, purpose, length of detention, the level of surveillance and other circumstances will all be relevant in deciding if the action amounts to deprivation of liberty, and so violates **A 5**. However, in **Ostendorf** and other cases these matters have been said to be relevant to whether the restriction comes within the exceptions, i.e., *after* a deprivation has been found (see under restrictions below).

There may be a deprivation of liberty in the case of detention in order to provide hospital treatment (as in **Cheshire** and **Storck**) but this is unlikely if it is in the person's best interest.

Case example

Evans and another v Alder Hey Children's NHS Foundation Trust 2018 involved **A 5** and also an application for a writ of *habeas corpus*. The parents wanted to take their terminally ill child to Italy for treatment. The medical evidence was compelling that he had a fatal and degenerative disease and he was on life support. As in **Bland**, the court made a declaration that support could lawfully be withdrawn as it was not in the child's best interests that it should continue. The parents said that preventing him being moved from the hospital interfered with his right to liberty under **A 5**. They applied for a writ of *habeas corpus*. The application was rejected and they appealed. The CA held that his detention was not a deprivation of liberty, but that even if it was it was lawful so did not violate **A 5**.

In addition, the writ of *habeas corpus* applied only to individuals unlawfully detained. As withdrawal of support had already been held to be lawful by a court of law the writ did not apply.

Restrictions on the right to liberty under the ECHR

Once it has been decided that there is a deprivation of liberty the court will consider whether it comes within one of the exceptions.

A 5 (1) provides that no one shall be deprived of his liberty *"save in the following cases and in accordance with a procedure prescribed by law"*. Briefly, these exceptions are:

a)   after conviction by a competent court
b)   for noncompliance with a court order or to secure the fulfilment of any obligation prescribed by law
c)   for the purpose of bringing the person before the competent legal authority on reasonable suspicion of having committed an offence or when it is reasonably considered necessary to prevent an offence or flight

Case examples

In **Guzzardi**, confinement on an island was a deprivation of liberty. However, it was a preventive measure not a punishment for a specific offence. It did not come within **A 5 (1)(a)** as a deprivation of liberty *"after conviction by a competent court"*. It did not come under **A 5 (1)(b)** as it was not prescribed by law. It was not **(c)** either as even if it was *"to prevent an offence or flight"* it was not for the purpose of bringing him before a legal authority.

In **Ostendorf**, the ECtHR held that **A 5** should not be interpreted in such a way as to make it impracticable for the police to fulfil their duties of maintaining order and protecting the public as long as they comply with the underlying principle of **A 5**, *"which is to protect the individual from arbitrariness"*. However, the words *"for the purpose of bringing him before the competent legal authority"* permitted only pre-trial detention and did not extend to preventative measures so did not satisfy **A 5 (1)(c)** despite the words *"to prevent an offence"*. There had been a deprivation of liberty but in finding there was no violation of **A 5** the ECtHR held that **A 5 (1)(b)** was satisfied because the police were fulfilling an obligation prescribed by law. However, opinion was divided on whether preventative measures were acceptable and this interpretation of **A 5 (1)** was not followed by the HL in **Austin**.

Task 8

A policeman sees two young boys, Sadiq and Khalid, coming out of a toy shop. Sadiq is carrying a rucksack and the policeman sees an unwrapped toy gun sticking out of it. He grabs both boys and tells them he is taking them to the police station. Can the boys claim that their rights under **A 5** have been violated?

Examination pointer

When looking at a scenario first consider whether there has been a deprivation of liberty using one or more of the ECtHR cases such as **Ostendorf** or **Guzzardi**. If not then **A 5** is not engaged at all and there is no need to look at the exceptions or to justify a breach. If in doubt, explain that **Austin** suggests that all the circumstances need to be considered when deciding whether the threshold is crossed and **A 5** engaged. Then note that the circumstances are also relevant when deciding whether any of the exceptions apply to allow the measures, and whether these are proportionate and not arbitrary.

A 5 (1)(c) allows for detention without charge, even though a person is supposedly innocent until found guilty in a court of law. However, under **A 5 (3)** everyone arrested or detained *"shall be brought promptly before a judge or other officer authorised by law to exercise judicial power and shall be entitled to trial within a reasonable time or to release pending trial. Release may be conditioned by guarantees to appear for trial."*

As well as restrictions **A 5 (2)** provides safeguards. These include that everyone who is arrested *"shall be informed promptly, in a language which he understands, of the reasons for his arrest"*. Failure to do this will make the arrest unlawful and so could amount to false imprisonment, as in **Christie v Leachinsky 1947**. If the person is touched while being detained unlawfully it could be a battery. This was the case in **Collins v Wilcock 1984**, where a police constable took hold of a woman's arm to question her, but as he had no power of arrest he committed a battery.

These provisions balance the rights and restrictions by allowing exceptions but offering safeguards to ensure a person is not detained longer than necessary.

The domestic courts are reluctant to allow the exceptions too widely, as seen in **Cheshire West and Chester Council v P 2014**, where the SC ruled that the right to liberty under **A 5** also applied to those without capacity to make their own decision and that any deprivation of liberty had to be necessary and in the person's best interest.

Whether restrictions on liberty are acceptable depends on the circumstances. An important factor is the length of detention, but this is not necessarily a defining factor. Others include the purpose (**Austin**), the amount of supervision (**Guzzardi**, **Cheshire**) and the size of the confinement area (**Guzzardi**).

Police custody, even if short-term, may engage **A 5** because locking someone up is the paradigm example of deprivation of liberty, as stated in **Austin**. This means duration is not relevant to whether the right is engaged in the first place, only to whether it is breached. Then it will be relevant to whether the measure was proportionate. However, the issue is not clear for situations outside this paradigm, as was the case in **Austin**.

- **Austin** suggests the circumstances are relevant to whether there is a deprivation of liberty
- **Ostendorf** suggests the circumstances are relevant to the exceptions
- **Guzzardi** appears to encompass both views

The decision in **Austin** appears to go against the ECtHR guide to **A 5**. This states that the purpose of the measures is not decisive for the assessment of whether there has been a deprivation of liberty but to whether that deprivation is compatible with **A 5**. This was the interpretation in **Ostendorf**.

There is also conflicting case law on whether **A 5** allows preventative measures. **Ostendorf** suggests that these can come within **A 5 (1)(b)** but not **(c)**.

Evaluation pointer

Ostendorf is arguably correct as **A 5 (1)(b)** allows restrictions for the fulfilment of any obligation prescribed by law. The prevention of violence and protection of the public are usually legal powers given to the police in most states. The argument that it should not come within **(c)** despite the words *"to prevent an offence"* is sustainable if read in context. The provision begins by stating *"for the purpose of bringing the person before the competent legal authority"*. So even if the restriction on liberty is reasonably considered necessary to prevent an offence there still has to be the ulterior motive of the intention of bringing the person before a competent legal authority.

Provisions in English law which impact on the right to liberty

Before going on to specific provisions, here are the questions to ask when considering whether a measure by a public authority violates a right:

- Does the measure interfere with a right under the **ECHR**?
- Under what English law is the measure allowed?
- Does any English law protect the right?

A claim may be under the specific English law e.g., negligence, or under **s 7 HRA** relying directly on the **ECHR** right in the case of interference by a public body.

Although a residual freedom rather than a right, liberty has long been important in England and is protected by the writ of *habeas corpus* (see Chapter 2). This meets the obligation under **A 5(3)** that a person detained *"shall be brought promptly before a judge"*. The writ is still used to challenge restrictions on the right to liberty and the right to a trial so meets the positive obligation to protect both these rights. It was seen in the **Alder Hey** case above where the parents applied for a writ in order to remove the child from hospital. The HC held their application to be *"misconceived"* because the issue had already been through the English courts up to the SC, so the application was merely an attempt to get a different decision on the same issue.

The greatest impact on the right to liberty comes from police powers to stop, search, detain and arrest an individual. These come under the **Police and Criminal Evidence Act 1984 (PACE)** as amended by the **Serious Organised Crime and Police Act 2005 (SOCPA)**, and the **Criminal Justice and Public Order Act 1994 (CJPOA)**. Police powers may breach the negative obligation not to interfere in the right but be justified as necessary to preserve order or protect others. In order to meet the positive obligation to protect the right to liberty under **A 5**, police powers are themselves subject to regulation under **PACE**, and the codes of practice which supplement it.

Police powers under PACE, SOCPA and CJPOA

- Powers to stop and search – under **s 1 PACE** the police can stop and search on reasonable suspicion that drugs, weapons or stolen or prohibited items may be found.
- Powers of arrest – under **s 24 PACE** (as amended by **s 110 SOCPA**) the police can arrest not only anyone who has committed or is committing an offence but also anyone who is about to commit an offence. There must be reasonable suspicion in each case.
- Powers of detention – several sections regulate detention. A custody officer should order the release of a prisoner if the reasons for detention have ceased to apply.

Prohibited items under **s 1** would include anything that could be used in theft or burglary so gives a wide discretion (a pair of gloves?). Under **s 2** the police must identify themselves, explain the object of the search and give reasons for making it. These matters must be formally recorded following the search under **s 3**.

As regards arrest there are similar safeguards. Under the amended **s 24** the police must identify themselves, tell you that you're being arrested and give reasons. These safeguards comply with the obligation under **A 5 (2)**. However, the police have wide powers to restrict liberty and prevent someone moving freely.

The **PACE** codes of practice balance these powers. Code of Practice A regulates stop and search powers. Code G regulates arrest and Code C covers detention and provides for limits on the time held, access to a solicitor, free legal advice and the right to have someone informed of the arrest. **S 34 PACE** provides that any detention should cease if there are no longer grounds for it or it cannot be justified. **S 41-43** provide further safeguards (as supplemented by Code G) as regards time limits and provisions for further detention.

Another provision that complies with the obligation to protect the right to liberty is that of granting bail. This allows for the release of the suspect pending further investigation and trial The **Bail Act 1976** governs the provision of bail. **S 4** provides that bail will be granted unless one of the exceptions in Schedule 1 applies. The main reasons to refuse bail are that the suspect may fail to surrender to custody, commit an offence while on bail, or interfere with witnesses. In most cases other than murder bail will be granted.

The provisions governing detention and bail comply with the obligation to protect the right to liberty and with the requirement under **A 5 (3)** that those detained should be *"entitled to trial within a reasonable time or to release pending trial"*. However, the section goes on to add *"Release may be conditioned by guarantees to appear for trial."* This allows release to be subject to bail.

S 60 CJPOA gives an additional power. It allows a senior officer to authorise searches for weapons in specified areas where serious violence is anticipated or dangerous implements or offensive weapons are suspected of being carried. This authorisation can last for up to 48 hours and gives a police constable power to stop any person or vehicle and search for weapons or dangerous instruments. The constable can *"make any search he thinks fit whether or not he has any grounds for suspecting that the person or vehicle is carrying weapons or articles of that kind"*.

Evaluation pointer

S 1 PACE provides stop and search powers but only where there is reasonable suspicion of various specified matters. **S 60 CJPOA** effectively allows for such powers to be used without this limit. Once the authorisation is granted it allows for searches within the designated area. Police powers of stop and search have always caused some controversy but the idea of a "suspicionless" search goes against the rule of law. People will not know that they are in a designated area and may therefore be the subject of such powers.

Case example

In **R (Roberts) v Commission of Police of the Metropolis 2015**, a woman had given a false name and address after refusing to pay a bus fare and the police were called. The area was known to be violent and was subject to an authorisation under **s 60**. She was acting nervously and clutching her bag as if she was concealing something. Even if this was not enough to give rise to reasonable suspicion the police had the power to search her bag for a weapon. She claimed violation of **A 5** and **A 8**. At first instance and in the CA it was accepted that the powers used were *"in accordance with the law"* and not disproportionate so her right to liberty had not been violated. Although she did not appeal against this **A 5** decision, a further appeal went to the SC on **A 8**, which was also rejected (see next chapter for more on **A 8**).

This was the first case on **s 60** to come before the SC or the ECtHR. However, the SC referred to earlier case law on other types of stop and search, e.g., under **PACE** as seen in **R (Gillan) v Commissioner of Police of the Metropolis 2006**. In that case Lord Bingham said that the exercise of power by public officials must be used only for the purpose for which it was given and should be governed by clear and accessible rules and not used arbitrarily (i.e., it must be compatible with the rule of law). He stated that any interference with, or derogation from, a right had to pass this test, calling the arbitrary use of power *"the antithesis of legality"*. On the facts in **Gillan**, the HL decided that a brief stop and search under the powers given by **s 60** did not conflict with the rule of law and did not violate **A 8**.

In **Roberts**, the SC agreed with this principle and noted that the requirement of legality under the **ECHR** meant *"more than mere compliance with the domestic law. It requires that the law be compatible with the rule of law"*. The SC noted the problem with **s 60** powers but decided that they were *"in accordance with the law"* in this sense so satisfied the legality requirement under **A 8**. The interference with her rights had been proportionate to the legitimate aim of the prevention of disorder or crime so was justified. This shows that there may be interference with a right but if it is justified there will be no violation. Although the appeal to the SC was on **A 8** rather than **A 5** the principle that the legality requirement requires more than mere adherence to domestic law applies across the **ECHR**. (An exception is A 2, although this allows taking a life where this penalty is *"provided by law"* the death penalty was abolished under English law long ago).

Here is how it applies to the other rights you need.

The legality requirement

A 5(1) provides that any interference with the right to liberty must be *"in accordance with a procedure prescribed by law"*

A 8(2) provides that any interference with the right to respect for a private life must be *"in accordance with law"*

A 10(2) and **A 11(2)** provide that any interference with the right to freedom of expression and freedom of assembly and association must be *"prescribed by law"*

The bit in italics in each right is the legality requirement. Case law such as **Gillan** and **Roberts** shows that not only must there be a domestic law allowing the interference, but also that any interference conforms to the rule of law. In addition, the measure must be proportionate to a legitimate aim. This may mean that it is justified in the circumstances.

Evaluation pointer

The arbitrary use of power is against the rule of law and, as Lord Bingham said, *"the antithesis of legality"*. It is good that any power which allows interference with rights under the **ECHR** should not be exercised arbitrarily. However, there are a huge number of laws which permit restrictions on **A 5** and this makes it hard for people to know how far their rights may be limited by state powers.

Other police powers and restrictions on liberty come under the **Public Order Act 1986** and the **Criminal Justice and Public Order Act 1994 (CJPOA)**. These mostly affect the right to freedom of assembly and association under **Article 11**, so to avoid repetition are discussed with that.

However, note that orders made to regulate assemblies will often restrict liberty so may impact on both rights.

Task 9

Lord Bingham said that the arbitrary use of power was *"the antithesis of legality"*. What did he mean and what rule does the arbitrary use of power violate?

Breach of the peace

Most police powers come under **PACE** but they also have power under English common law to arrest and detain anyone who is committing, or they have reasonable cause to believe is about to commit, a breach of the peace. Breach of the peace is not a crime in itself, but the police can apply for a court order to bind the person over to keep the peace and be of good behaviour. Non-compliance with this order would then be an offence. An arrest for an anticipated breach of the peace will only be lawful if the threat of a breach is imminent but these powers have the potential to conflict with **A 5, 10** and **11**.

Case examples

The ECtHR decision in **Austin** was followed in the UK domestic court in **R (on the application of Moos) v Commissioner of Police for the Metropolis 2012** when the CA allowed an appeal by the police against a HC ruling that their actions in using kettling to control Climate Camp protesters during a G 20 summit breached **A 5**. The CA stated that whether a breach of the peace was imminent was a matter for the police to decide. There must be a reasonable cause to fear a breach in order to justify restraining someone's liberty, but this was the case here. In **Austin** the HL held that the confinement was *"not the kind of arbitrary deprivation of liberty that is proscribed by the Convention, so article 5(1) was not applicable"*. The ECtHR agreed that it did not engage **A 5** in the first place rather than that it breached **A 5** but was justified.

Note that where protesters are detained **A 5** is appropriate, but **A 11** also comes into play because the group is an assembly.

In **R (on the application of Hicks and others) v Commissioner of Police for the Metropolis 2017**, the SC considered the restrictions under **A 5** as regards both time (short) and purpose (to prevent a breach of the peace). Four individuals had been arrested and detained in police cells on the day of the wedding of the Duke and Duchess of Cambridge. Their arrest was clearly a deprivation of liberty (the paradigm case referred to in **Austin**) and the police considered there was a risk of a breach of the peace so the arrest was reasonably believed to be necessary. The period of detention was between two and five and a half hours and they were all released without charge once the wedding was over. Unlike **Austin** there was a deprivation of liberty so the SC looked at the exceptions.

The applicants argued that they were not detained *"for the purpose of"* bringing them before a legal authority. The SC held that it would be absurd to suggest a short-term detention, where there was no time to bring a person before the court, would violate the right to liberty. That would mean in order not to violate **A 5** the police would have to hold the person longer (i.e., until such a time a court appearance was possible). The SC noted that opinion in **Ostendorf** was divided on whether **A 5 (1)(c)** allowed preventative measures and preferred the minority view that it did (the majority decision was based on A **5 (1)(b)**). The SC agreed that the underlying principle of **A 5** is to protect the individual from arbitrariness. This requires that judicial supervision is available, but should not mean making it impracticable for the police to maintain public order. The SC held that the measures were proportionate in the circumstances (which included protecting the public), were not arbitrary and did not breach **A 5**.

Evaluation pointer

I said in the earlier pointer that **Ostendorf** seems correct that preventative measures can come within **A 5 (1)(b)** but not **(c)**. However, **Hicks** suggests that preventative measures can come within **(c)** as well and this also has its merits. **A 5 (1)(c)** allows for the detention of a person *"for the purpose of bringing him before the competent legal authority"*. It seems sensible to be able to arrest someone for a short time to prevent disorder or violence because doing so for longer is allowed if it is to give time to arrange a court appearance. Anyway, at the time of the arrest there may be intention to do this but that intention may change as evidence clarifies the issue. **A 5 (1)(c)** appears to be a matter of intent rather than action. If this is the case then if the police intend to bring a suspect before a court that should suffice, even if they then let the suspect go.

Note that it had been decided by the ECtHR (in **Steel v UK 1998**) that although a breach of the peace is not an offence in English law it counts as one for the purposes of the **A 5**. This was confirmed by the SC in **Hicks**.

A 5 allows for a restriction on liberty *"to secure the fulfilment of any obligation prescribed by law"*. The prevention of a breach of the peace is probably the most common example of this and a part of English common law long before **A 5**. In **Hicks 2017**, Lord Toulson said *"The power of the police, or any other citizen, to carry out an arrest to prevent an imminent breach of the peace is ancient, but it remains as relevant today as in times past"*.

As to what amounts to a breach of peace, the definition comes from **Howell 1981** where the HC stated that it requires *"an act done or threatened to be done which either actually harms a person, or in his presence his property, or is likely to cause such harm, or which puts someone in fear of such harm being done"*.

Remember that whether there is a deprivation of liberty is one of degree. Locking someone in a prison cell is a clear example of a deprivation. In other situations the circumstances will need to be carefully looked at. In **Guzzardi** confining someone to an island was a deprivation of liberty under **A 5**. In **Austin** confining people by the use of kettling was not. If there is no deprivation of liberty then **A 5** is not engaged at all. It is not a question of breaching the right and then justifying the breach. However, there is some conflict between **Austin** and **Ostendorf**. In **Austin** there was no deprivation whereas in **Ostendorf** there was a deprivation but it was justified.

Examination pointer

It is useful to know a few cases where opinions differed as it will allow you to be unsure in your application. Thus, if the scenario involved someone being stopped from leaving an area this could be similar to kettling (so acceptable following **Austin**) but the circumstances could make it nearer to being locked up, e.g., if in a small area and for a long time with constant supervision (so not acceptable following **Guzzardi**). Also the fact that the law is not clear as regards at what stage you need to consider the circumstances means you can point to **Austin** and **Ostendorf** and say *"there may not be any interference with the right because it was short-term and the purpose was to prevent violence (Austin), but if there is then the circumstances need to be looked at (Ostendorf) ..."* and go on to discuss whether there is a breach or whether the interference is justified. The English courts appear to favour the **Ostendorf** ruling, as seen in **Hicks**.

Derogation and A 5 (3)

Under **A 5 (3)** everyone arrested or detained under **A 5 (1)** *"shall be brought promptly before a judge or other officer authorised by law to exercise judicial power"*. **A 15** allows for derogation from this if there is a public emergency threatening the life of the nation and the powers granted were necessary and proportionate in the situation. The UK used this derogation during the conflict in Northern Ireland in the 1970s and early 1980s to opt out of **A 5 (3)** in order to detain terrorists without a trial. It was accepted that the circumstances in Northern Ireland met the criteria for derogation so allowed for the preventative detention of terrorist suspects without trial.

In **Brogan v UK 1988** the applicants had been held for periods of up to a week without charge or trial on suspicion of terrorist activities. The ECtHR held that as the government had withdrawn the notice of derogation **A 15** could not be considered. However, the British government were not in breach of **A 5 (1)** because at the time of detention the suspects had been detained *"for the purpose of"* bringing them before a competent legal authority. There was breach of **A 5 (3)** however, because they had not been brought *"promptly"* before a judge. Even the shortest time of four days was too wide an interpretation of promptly.

(Note that the UK derogated from **A 5 (1)** when it passed the **HRA** but this provision was repealed in 2005.)

In **A v the Home Department 2005**, known as the 'Belmarsh case' after the prison where suspects were held, several suspects had been held for three years without trial. This was permitted under English law and they argued breach of **A 5**. The UK argued the law was necessary to protect the life of the nation. The HL accepted there was a threat so the first part of **A 15** was satisfied but said the response to that threat (to hold suspects without charge indefinitely) was not *"necessary and proportionate"*. One issue was that it only applied to foreigners not to a national posing the same threat. Lord Hoffman said that terrorism had succeeded if it meant the country rejected the rule of law in response to threats of terrorism.

The English law was declared incompatible under **s 4 HRA**. The case went to the ECtHR in 2009 and the court agreed that the HL decision was correct.

Task 10

The HL held that the Act was against the rule of law. Explain three aspects to this rule.

The courts do not favour individual rights over the public interest if the restriction on the freedom is less severe. In **Beghal v DPP 2015**, a woman was stopped by police on arrival at East Midlands airport and questioned for several hours. There were no grounds for suspicion other than that her husband was in custody in France on charges of terrorism. However, the **Terrorism Act 2000** allowed the action in stopping her and asking questions. She argued that this conflicted with her rights under **A 5**. The case went to the SC which held that the actions of detaining her were both proportionate and legitimate and that most international travellers expected some kind of interference with their rights in the interests of safety. The case makes some important points. Firstly, the SC confirmed the legality requirement included conforming to the rule of law. Secondly, it noted that legality is a prior test designed to ensure any interference can be proportionate. Finally, it restated what questions should be asked to establish this proportionality. These are:

- is the objective sufficiently important to justify limitation upon a fundamental right?
- is the measure rationally connected to the objective?
- could a less intrusive measure have been adopted?
- has a fair balance been struck between individual rights and the interests of the community?

The SC also noted that *"two fundamental and well-established functions of any government are the defence of the realm from external attack and the maintenance of the rule of law internally"*.

Task 11

A crowd of people had gathered on the day of a royal wedding. Many of the people were anti-monarchy and the crowd were getting angry. The police were concerned there would be violence and arrested several of those involved. Tanya and Mo were held for four hours until the wedding was over and the risk of violence had reduced. Jed was held overnight and released the next morning. No charges were brought against any of those held. Discuss whether their rights under **A 5** had been violated.

Balancing conflicting interests and the rule of law: Terrorism is useful for illustrating balancing conflicting interests and justice and is of particular importance when discussing the rule of law. In addition, cases such as **Beghal** make important points on human rights law generally, especially on justifying interference. Here is a bit more detail.

In the **Belmarsh** case, the UK had recognised it was in breach of **A 5** but argued that the provision for detention under the **Act** was justified under **A 15**. The HL held that the two matters to consider were first whether there was a threat and secondly whether the response to that threat was both *"necessary and proportionate"*. The majority thought the first was satisfied but not the second. The **Act** was declared incompatible under **s 4 HRA 1998**.

The effect of this was that, even though the judgment was not enforceable, changes were made to the law. The **Prevention of Terrorism Act 2005** provided for relocation, tagging, up to 16 hours curfew, regular reporting to the police and house arrest as an alternative to detention and restricted the use of mobile phones and the internet. The **2005 Act** was criticised as breaching **A 5** as although not technically imprisoning suspected terrorists the controls allowed for deprivation of liberty without charge and were based purely on 'reasonable suspicion', which is easily satisfied and too low a standard of proof for a criminal case. The control orders were abolished by the **Terrorism Prevention and Investigation Measures Act 2011**. These reduced the controls but still allow for tagging and reporting to the police so terrorist suspects continue to be dealt without outside the legal system.

The **Terrorism Act 2006** removed the indefinite detention but still allowed for suspects to be held without charge for 28 days. This was increased to 42 days by the **Counter-Terrorism Act 2008**. The **Protection from Freedom Act 2012** has reduced it to 14 days.

The amount of legislation which followed the **Belmarsh** case illustrates the difficulties of protecting both the public interest and individual rights. The various Acts have changed some of the worst excesses but have put public interests above private. The American jurist, Roscoe Pound, said that interests on a different level should not be balanced because attempting to balance public and private interests would always result in the public interests prevailing. This may be the case but many would argue that it is necessary. The interests of society in wanting to be protected have to be balanced not only against the suspect's rights, but also against the other interests of society in living in a free and fair state, and of justice as a whole and the need to uphold the rule of law. However, although we all want to be safe, most people do not want to live in a society that can lock people up without any charges being brought against them. A criminal trial is the proper place to decide these issues.

Task 12

Briefly explain the facts of **Beghal** and why her action under **A 5** failed.

Another English law which has led to challenge and calls for reform is the law on insanity. There have been claims that the **M'Naghten** Rules for establishing insanity violate **A 5**. Although **A 5** is a limited right and allows the lawful detention of persons of unsound mind, it is arguable that people who suffer from epilepsy or diabetes do not come within this description. Also the potential indeterminate sentence in a mental hospital for someone who has been found '*not guilty* by reason of insanity' is against the right to liberty. Northern Ireland has amended the law to avoid incompatibility but English law is still based on the common law rules established in **M'Naghten**. **A 5** also states that a person of unsound mind can only be detained where proper objective medical expertise has been sought. This was mentioned in the introduction to the Law Commission's 2012 project on insanity as one of the reasons for the need to reform the law.

Summary of provisions that impact on A 5

- A 5 (2) provisions
- Custodial sentence by a court
- Police powers under PACE
- Refusal of bail
- Police powers under SOCPA
- Police powers under Public Order Act

Article 5 — the right to liberty

The right to a fair hearing under Article 6

Article 6 (1) provides:

In the determination of his civil rights and obligations or of any criminal charge against him, everyone is entitled to a fair and public hearing within a reasonable time by an independent and impartial tribunal established by law. Judgment shall be pronounced publicly but the press and public may be excluded from all or part of the trial in the interests of morals, public order or national security in a democratic society, where the interests of juveniles or the protection of the private life of the parties so require, or to the extent strictly necessary in the opinion of the court in special circumstances where publicity would prejudice the interests of justice.

Task 13

A 6 provides that there must be a *"fair and public hearing within a reasonable time by an independent and impartial tribunal"*. Briefly explain the importance of an independent judiciary.

One example of **A 6** that you have already seen is the case of **Thompson and Venables 1999**. Here the trial of two young boys in an adult court was held to be in breach of **A 6**. The effect of this judgment of the ECtHR was that special procedures were established for youth trials

A 6 imposes a positive duty on the state to protect the right to a fair hearing. Provisions that grant the right to a solicitor and other procedural rights under **PACE** and the **Access to Justice Act** are there to ensure a person has a fair trial and to comply with this obligation. The negative obligation is not to interfere with the right and this could be violated by not providing for youth trials (as in **Thompson and Venables**) or not allowing the accused to cross-examine a witness (as in **Davis 2008** below). Lack of access to legal aid and assistance may also impact on **A 6**.

In **Ibrahim and others v. the UK 2016**, four people who had been arrested following the London bombings in 2001 finally had their case heard in the ECtHR. They argued that their rights under **A 6** had been breached because they were not properly cautioned and were denied access to legal advice. Three had their petitions dismissed as they were arrested on suspicion of terrorism while there was still fear of a serious danger to the public, so speed was paramount. The measure was justified so there had been no violation of **A 6**. However, the fourth was being questioned as a witness and had not been arrested when he started to incriminate himself, so he should have been cautioned and offered legal advice. The ECtHR held that his right to a fair trial had been prejudiced and there was no justification in his case.

Task 14

You can see that there is an overlap between **A 5** and **A 6**. Look back at the facts in Task 11 and briefly explain whether the **A 6** rights of Tanya, Mo and Jed would have been breached if they had not been allowed access to a solicitor.

Under **A 6(2)** everyone is presumed innocent until proved guilty. **A 6(3)** provides other safeguards which include the right to be informed about the nature of the accusation, time to prepare a defence, to examine witnesses and to have free legal assistance if that is in the interests of justice. Again, you can see an overlap with **A 5**, in particular with police powers and the **PACE** codes of practice. In **Murray v UK 1996** denying a prisoner access to a solicitor for 48 hours was found to be in breach of **A 6**.

In **Davis 2008** a man argued that he could not have fair trial where witnesses had been granted anonymity because he would not be able to cross-examine them. The HL agreed that he should have the right to question those who made allegations against him so his right outweighed both the public interest (in protecting witnesses from intimidation) and the private interests of the witnesses themselves. The UK law allowing witness anonymity breached **A 6**.

The UK government responded by rushing emergency legislation through Parliament. The **Criminal Evidence (Witness Anonymity) Act 2008** allowed anonymity for vulnerable witnesses or where anonymity was necessary to prevent intimidation. ,This is now included in the **Coroners and Justice Act 2009** but there is a proviso that anonymity should only be given where this is consistent with a defendant's right to a fair trial, thus keeping in line with **A 6**.

In **Horncastle 2009** the SC declined to follow a decision of the ECtHR in **Al-Khawaja 2009**. This was a similar issue in that the witnesses were not in court so could not be cross-examined. This is allowed under procedural rules on the use of hearsay evidence in the English courts. The ECtHR in **Al-Khawaja** had held that if the conviction was based solely on such evidence it was a breach of **A 6**. The SC, in **Horncastle**, declined to follow this and held it did not breach **A 6**. In **Al-Khawaja 2011** the ECtHR held that while **A 6** would normally require that there is an opportunity to challenge the evidence, this was not an absolute. The question would be whether there are sufficient measures in place that would allow a proper assessment of the reliability of that evidence. The ECtHR decided in line with the SC showing that the courts have a dialogue between them and are not in opposition. Another SC case involving **A 6** is **Maguire 2018**. The accused had been granted legal aid for two barristers but there was a procedural problem with one and he was unable to appear as leading counsel. The accused argued that this breached his right under **A 6**. The HC rejected this argument and the SC rejected his appeal. Although the right to a fair trial may require access to legal representation it did not extend to insisting on a particular barrister at public expense.

Restrictions on Article 6 and the impact of English law provisions

A 6 provides for the right to a fair and public hearing. However, the provision continues "*but the press and public may be excluded from all or part of the trial in the interests of morals, public order or national security in a democratic society, where the interests of juveniles or the protection of the private life of the parties so require, or to the extent strictly necessary in the opinion of the court in special circumstances where publicity would prejudice the interests of justice*". The right to a fair trial is not limited to any great extent but **A 6** allows for the press and public to be excluded in certain circumstances.

The summary of what you need to look for when applying the law applies here too so look back at the introduction to the English provisions for **A 5** but for a fair and public hearing rather than deprivation of liberty.

National provisions have been covered to an extent with the safeguards discussed above. Others would include legal procedures which regulate bail, trial procedures, juries, access to justice etc.

Examples

In **Thompson and Venables 1999** the trial of two young boys in an adult court was held to be in breach of **A 6**. This case was heard in the ECtHR and the result was that special procedures were established for youth trials.

In **Davis 2008** the HL held that the UK had breached **A 6** because the law allowed for witness anonymity. The UK government responded by rushing emergency legislation through Parliament to allow this, although in more limited circumstances.

When the right to silence was effectively abolished in the UK under **s 34** of the **CJPOA**, there were several challenges to this. If a suspect being questioned failed to mention something later relied on in court, **s 34** allowed the court to draw "*such inferences from the failure as appear proper*". The challenges therefore relied on the right to a fair trial under **A 6**. In **Murray v UK 1996** the ECtHR ruled that **s 34** did not violate **A 6**. Unlike the situation in America, where the right to silence is a fundamental right under the US Constitution, no such right exists in the UK, where the law is based on residual freedoms rather than rights. However, in the same case, the ECtHR ruled that denying a prisoner access to a solicitor for 48 hours was in breach of **A 6**. In deciding whether **A 6** is breached in such situations, much will depend on the facts. The length of time will be one such factor. However, note that in 2003, an addition to **CJPOA** provided that **s 34** does not apply if the accused was at an authorised place of detention at the time of the failure and had not been allowed access to a solicitor prior to being questioned.

In **Foye 2013**, the CA considered the rule in **s 2** of the **Homicide Act 1957** that the burden of establishing diminished responsibility lies with the defendant, on the balance of probabilities (rather than with the prosecution beyond reasonable doubt which is the norm in criminal cases). The CA concluded that this was not incompatible with the presumption of innocence contained in **A 6(2)**.

There is a significant overlap between **A 5** and **A 6**, e.g., terrorism cases have often involved both a denial of liberty and denial of a right to a fair trial. Look back at the provisions which impact on **A 5** for more on this and see the Belmarsh case for an example.

In **Gillan** Lord Bingham said that the exercise of power by public officials must be used only for the purpose for which it was given and should be governed by clear and accessible rules and not used arbitrarily. This applies to all restrictions on the rights but has been referred to in many terrorism cases where detention or lack of a fair trial has been decided on without consideration of the individual circumstances.

Task 15

Imran is a police officer on duty in Gorby, an area known to be violent and subject to an authorisation under **s 60 Criminal Justice and Public Order Act 1994**. He sees Marlese in a shop doorway; she is acting nervously and seems to be hiding something in her bag. He takes her to the police van and searches her bag for weapons. He finds nothing but she has been swearing at him and calling him racist names, so he keeps her locked in the van for three hours before he lets her go.

Advise Marlese whether she might have a claim under **A 5** or **A 6**.

Summary of provisions that impact on A 6

- A 6 (1) provisions
- bail
- witness anonymity
- access to a solicitor
- Article 6 the right to a fair trial
- jury secrecy
- special provisions for youth trials
- the right to silence

Self-test questions

1. What is the paradigm example of a deprivation of liberty?
2. What is the main difference between A 5 (1) and (3)?
3. In Beghal what questions did the SC say should be asked to establish proportionality
4. In which case was the trial of two young boys in an adult court held to be in breach of **A 6**?
5. In which case did the SC decline to follow a decision of the ECtHR?

Chapter 4 Rights and restrictions under Articles 8, 10 and 11 of the ECHR

The rights in **A 8**, **10** and **11** are qualified and the state has a wide margin of appreciation (discretion) in how to interpret and protect them. Interference can be justified if necessary in a democratic society. To be justified the interference must be proportionate to a legitimate aim. There are numerous English law provisions which impact on these rights and many apply to more than right. To avoid too much repetition the rights and restrictions are covered in this chapter and the English law provisions in the next (though you will see examples here too). Application tasks are in the next chapter.

The right to respect for private and family life under Article 8

A 8 (1) provides:

Everyone has the right to respect for his private and family life, his home and his correspondence.

This is an extremely wide-ranging right and cases cover the withdrawal of medical treatment, the force-feeding of an anorexic, the smoking ban in prisons, allowing children who are "Gillick competent" to make decisions for themselves, telephone hacking and data protection. Here is a table of examples from my book on *"The nature of law for OCR"*.

The aspect of private life involved	Case examples
The storage of embryos for fertilisation at a later date	Jefferies 2016
The right to die	Nicklinson & Another 2014 / Conway v SS for Justice 2017
The withdrawal of treatment	Re M 2011 / M v A Hospital 2017 / PL 2017
The force-feeding of an anorexic	Re E 2012
The smoking ban in prisons	Black v the Secretary of State for Justice 2015
Allowing children who are "Gillick competent" to make decisions for themselves	Gillick v West Norfolk and Wisbech AHA 1986 / Axon v Secretary of State for Health 2006
Data protection	Home Secretary v Tom Watson & Others 2016 / Andrew v MPC 2017

The table gives a few examples of what issues could come within **A 8**. If you are interested in knowing more, you can refer to the book or look them up.

What is the right to a private and family life?

The ECtHR guide says:

"Although the object of Article 8 is essentially that of protecting the individual against arbitrary interference by the public authorities, it does not merely compel the State to abstain from such interference: in addition to this primarily negative undertaking, there may be positive obligations inherent in an effective respect for private life. These obligations may involve the

adoption of measures designed to secure respect for private life even in the sphere of the relations of individuals between themselves".

This means the state has a negative obligation not to interfere with the right to respect for a private and family life, e.g., by intrusive surveillance or indiscriminate collection and retention of data. It also has a positive obligation to protect the right. The latter may mean taking measures to regulate dealings between individuals in order to protect the right. The first example is of the positive duty and the second of the negative one.

Examples

In **Von Hannover v Germany 2012**, Princess Caroline of Monaco argued her rights under **A 8** had been breached by publication of photographs of her and her children. There were several cases in both the German courts and the ECtHR over many years but the final case was based on the argument that the German courts had not protected her **A 8** rights. The ECtHR held that Germany had not violated her rights because the court had granted an injunction against some private photographs being printed and had taken the correct matters into account in allowing publication of others. In particular, the court had considered the important question of whether the photographs had contributed to a debate of general public interest. In this instance there was a genuine public interest in the princess and her family which the German court had correctly taken into account. The ECtHR drew a distinction between the publication of photographs which concerned private matters and those which concerned public matters. **A 8** was concerned with protecting the former and the German state had done this.

In **Peck v UK 2003**, the council had released CCTV footage to parts of the media as part of a security programme. The footage showed images of the applicant. The ECtHR held that the disclosures were not accompanied by sufficient safeguards so constituted an unjustified interference with his private life and a violation of **A 8**.

The state also has a duty to protect people's identity and sexuality and not to discriminate. The ECtHR has frequently referred to the **ECHR** as a living instrument. This means the courts should take into account the circumstances such as technological advances and changing social values. One area where human rights law has evolved is regarding sexuality. In **Rees v UK 1986** (female-to-male transsexual) and **Cossey v UK 1993** (male-to-female transsexual), the ECtHR held transsexuals were not protected by **A 8** as such matters came within the states' margin of appreciation.

In **Goodwin v UK 2002**, the ECtHR made clear that this is no longer the case and held that the "*very essence*" of the **ECHR** is respect for human dignity and freedom.

Case examples

In **Bellinger v Bellinger 2003**, the HL declared that the **Matrimonial Causes Act 1973 (MCA)** was incompatible with **A 8** because it prevented transsexuals from marrying. The HL also held that it could not interpret the English law to comply with the **ECHR**. As the law stood, gender was decided at birth so people who had changed gender could not marry because the marriage was not between a man and a woman as required by the **MCA**. The following case went to the ECtHR just before the HL ruling in **Bellinger**.

In **Goodwin v UK 2002**, the ECtHR ruled that the UK law which prevented transsexuals from marrying breached **A 8**. This led to the **Gender Recognition Act 2004**, so that the English law now recognises the acquired gender rather than the gender at birth and complies with **A 8**.

In **ADT v UK 2000**, the ECtHR ruled that the offence of gross indecency in English law breached **A 8** because it only applied to homosexual activities. In **B v UK 2004**, the ECtHR ruled that homosexuals should not be treated differently to heterosexuals and that having different ages for consent to sexual activity was in breach of **A 8** and **A 14** which prohibits discrimination. The **Civil Partnership Act 2004** allowed for partnerships between homosexual couples to be legally recognised and in 2014 gay marriage became legal when **s 1** of the **Marriage (Same Sex Couples) Act 2013** came into force. This was meant to equalise the rights of heterosexuals and gays. However, it resulted in inequality because now same-sex couples had two choices where heterosexual couples only had the marriage option. The **Civil Partnership Act** was challenged by a heterosexual couple who argued breach of **A 8**. The CA rejected their challenge but in **R (on the application of Steinfeld and Keidan) v Secretary of State for International Development 2018** the SC ruled that it was incompatible with both **A 14** (on discrimination) and **A 8**. The government accepted the law was incompatible but tried to justify it remaining in place by saying time was needed to decide how to move forward. Lord Kerr rejected this argument saying it could not be *"characterised as a legitimate aim"*. A declaration of incompatibility with both articles was made under **s 4 HRA**.

The right to a private and family life imposes obligations on the state to protect human dignity. We also saw in **Fadeyeva v. Russia 2003** that protection of physical integrity comes under **A 8**. As noted earlier, it is extremely wide-ranging.

A 8 is relevant to situations where someone is subject to long-term detention, e.g., in prison or hospital. This is because the institution is effectively home, so the right to respect for a private and family life comes into play.

Case examples

In **Dickson v UK 2007** a couple had been refused IVF treatment because one was in prison. They argued that this contravened their right to family life. The ECtHR held that prisoners' had rights and these were not forfeited on conviction. The UK policy of refusing treatment was not justified so breached **A 8**.

In **Black v the Secretary of State for Justice 2015**, a prisoner claimed that the law was wrong to allow smoking in prisons when it was banned elsewhere. He said that secondary smoking affected his health and the policy breached his right to a private life under **A 8**. The CA rejected his argument and held that the government should have time to bring the policy into effect gradually. A compulsory ban brought in suddenly could cause discipline and security problems. The policy was therefore justified in the interests of public safety. The smoking ban came into force in prisons in 2017.

Task 16

Explain the term margin of appreciation and when it can be used.

In **W v Secretary of State for Justice 2017**, (heard with several other appeals), the applicants challenged the UK scheme under which past convictions have to be disclosed when applying for particular employment. The courts considered two issues.

- Whether the scheme is *"in accordance with law"* and
- Whether it is *"necessary in a democratic society in the interests of national security, public safety etc."*

The CA held that a conviction for ABH having to be disclosed some 31 years after the event was incompatible with **A 8**. The rights of individuals to put their past behind them have to be balanced against the needs of society to ensure that the public are kept safe from those who might remain a risk. An important factor was the lack of safeguards to prevent the arbitrary use of the scheme, e.g., the opportunity to have the decision reviewed in individual cases. This is true of much human rights law. A state is more likely to be in violation of the **ECHR** where there is no access to the courts or other independent review of the policy or scheme being challenged. As Lord Bingham said, arbitrariness is the antithesis of legality.

Restrictions on A 8

Qualified rights not only allow the state a wider margin of appreciation as to how far they must be protected but also the **ECHR** provides exceptions in paragraph two of each Article.

Article 8 (2) states:

There shall be no interference by a public authority with the exercise of this right except such as is in accordance with the law and is necessary in a democratic society in the interests of national security, public safety or the economic well-being of the country, for the prevention of disorder or crime, for the protection of health or morals, or for the protection of the rights and freedoms of others.

This means that individual rights may be sacrificed in the public interest, e.g., state security or to protect health. There must be a domestic law allowing the measure and it must be necessary. In deciding what is necessary, the courts will need to consider if the measure was justified and will take into account whether it was proportionate in relation to a legitimate aim to be achieved.

In **Roberts 2015**, we saw that the CA held that any interference with her **A 8** rights had been *"in accordance with the law"* (**s 60 CJPOA**), and was justified because it was proportionate to a legitimate aim (the prevention of crime). Here are three examples from the ECtHR.

Case examples

In **Gard and others v UK 2017**, the ECtHR rejected complaints by a child's parents about a hospital withdrawing treatment against their wishes. The challenge was based on rights under **Articles 2**, **5**, **6** and **8**. The ECtHR accepted that rights under **A 8** had been interfered with but held that the interference had been necessary in a democratic society, in accordance with the law and pursued a legitimate aim.

In **Barbulescu v Romania 2017**, the ECtHR held an employer had breached **A 8** when sacking a worker for sending private messages on work social media. This does not mean an employer cannot restrict and monitor usage; the point is that such actions must be proportionate to any aims, and employees should be told they may be monitored.

In **Peck v UK 2003**, the ECtHR held that the disclosure of the CCTV footage pursued the legitimate aim of public safety etc. but the lack of sufficient safeguards meant the measures were a disproportionate and therefore an unjustified interference with his private life.

The right to freedom of expression under Article 10

A 10 (1) provides:

Everyone has the right to freedom of expression. This right shall include freedom to hold opinions and to receive and impart information and ideas without interference by public authority and regardless of frontiers

Most democracies allow freedom of expression. The right to speak freely and hold opinions which may be against the government of the day or other authorities has long been valued by those who believe in the importance of an open society. This is especially true with freedom of the press and other media, which is necessary in a democracy to ensure information is widely available.

What is freedom of expression?

On the ECtHR website the guide to A 10 says:

"The basic approach taken in Article 10 is to define freedom of expression very broadly, so as to include almost every form of expressive activity, and also to define very broadly what constitutes an interference with the enjoyment of this right, thus casting an extremely wide prima facie net of protection. Certain interferences with this right are justifiable under Article 10, so that Contracting States may legitimately impose restrictions on the right, for example to protect other rights or overriding interests, such as national security".

The guide also notes that the right covers *"not only information and ideas which are widely held but also minority viewpoints and views that many people might find offensive. Indeed, it is in relation to precisely this speech that the right is arguably most important"*. This point was reinforced in **Gillberg v Sweden 2012** where the ECtHR said freedom of expression was essential in a democratic society and applied not only to inoffensive information and ideas *"but also to those that offend, shock or disturb"*.

The right is therefore extremely wide-ranging and interference may be harder to justify.

The state has a positive obligation to protect freedom of expression, especially minority viewpoints. It also has a negative obligation not to interfere with this right e.g., by laws restricting free speech. Freedom of expression includes the right to receive information as well as communicate it. This makes sense because without the ability to know the facts there is no freedom to pass them on. Requests under the **Freedom of Information Act 2000** would therefore come under **A 10**. In order to produce accurate information on what the government, or other public authority, is doing, the media will need access to state information and statistics. Similarly, people who want to challenge government decisions need to know what those decisions are based on. However, the right to receive information does not mean there is a positive obligation on the state to provide it, only a negative obligation not to restrict others giving it out. This has been the subject of several cases where people have argued that the negative obligation on the state not to restrict access had a counterpart right for individuals to have access to it. This argument has not yet been wholly successful.

Case example

In **Roche v UK 2005** a man had requested records from the army to support a claim for a pension based on exposure to chemicals while he was serving in the army. The state had not provided the records and the case ended up in the ECtHR. The ECtHR held that **A 10** imposes a negative obligation on the state not to restrict a person from receiving information that others wish to impart, but does not impose a positive obligation to give out information. The state had therefore not breached **A 10** by not releasing the army records.

This point had been made clear much earlier, in **Leander v Sweden 1987**. This case was referred to in **Roche** when the ECtHR decided there was no positive obligation on the state to release information. However, more recent cases have raised arguments that the law had broadened since then towards the recognition of a right of access to information. This has not been fully clarified.

In **Gillberg v Sweden 2012** the ECtHR stated that *"the right to receive and impart information explicitly forms part of the right to freedom of expression under article 10. That right basically prohibits a Government from restricting a person from receiving information that others wish or may be willing to impart to him"*. The case was somewhat complex but involved an employee of a public university denying access to research material. He argued he had a right under **A 10** to refuse access to protect the people used in the research. In rejecting his argument the court held that it would restrict the rights of others to receive the information. This suggests there is such a right, but the matter was not determined.

That decisions of the ECtHR have not been entirely consistent was noted by the SC in **Kennedy v Charity Commission 2014** when it held that to depart from **Leander** in a way which makes disclosure of information by a public body obligatory would need a clearer decision (see next chapter for this case).

One factor that the ECtHR has referred to in cases involving the press (e.g., **Von Hannover**) is their *"watchdog role"* which is necessary in a democratic society. This will be a significant factor in cases where a journalist is requesting information. It was mentioned in **Kennedy** but the UK law was too clear (and the ECtHR law not clear enough). In **Gillberg v Sweden** the ECtHR rejected his argument that he was in the same position as a journalist protecting his sources. The court made clear that journalists have stronger rights under **A 10** because they act as watchdogs in a democratic society.

Task 17

Can you think of three examples of when you might want to claim a right to freedom of expression? What restrictions do you think might be imposed on your chosen rights?

Restrictions on A 10

Article 10 (2) states:

The exercise of these freedoms, since it carries with it duties and responsibilities, may be subject to such formalities, conditions, restrictions or penalties as are prescribed by law and are necessary in a democratic society, in the interests of national security, territorial integrity or public safety, for the prevention of disorder or crime, for the protection of health or morals, for the protection of the reputation or rights of others, for preventing the disclosure of information received in confidence, or for maintaining the authority and impartiality of the judiciary.

Case example

In **Miranda v Home Department 2016** the CA referred to **Beghal** but held that **A 10** imposed different obligations. A journalist had been stopped and questioned at Heathrow and material was taken from him. This contained encrypted data given to him by Edward Snowden (who had stolen it from the National Security Agency of the United States). Much of the material came from the intelligence services at GCHQ in the UK and contained information that could damage state security. The stop and detention were allowed under the **Terrorism Act 2000**.

Miranda claimed this breached his rights under **A 10**. The CA restated the proportionality principle that a fair balance had to be struck between the rights of the individual and the interests of the community. The greater the potential harm, the greater the weight that should be accorded to the community interests. On the facts, the CA held that the action was not disproportionate to the aim of preventing classified material reaching the public domain and endangering security. However, the CA issued a declaration of incompatibility with **A 10** under **s 4 HRA** because there were inadequate safeguards against the arbitrary exercise of the power, such as prior judicial or other independent and impartial scrutiny. The stop was therefore not *"prescribed by law"* as required by **A 10 (2)**. This again shows that a state is more likely to be in violation where there is no opportunity to have the decision independently reviewed in individual cases.

S 12 HRA strengthens **A 10** as it specifically requires courts and tribunals to consider the importance of **A 10** in any case where it may be restricted. **S 12** imposes an obligation to *"have particular regard to the importance of the Convention right to freedom of expression"* where the material published is *"journalistic, literary or artistic"*. The courts will therefore look carefully at any restrictions on freedom of expression where such material is involved.

The right to freedom of peaceful assembly and association under Article 11

A 11(1) provides:

"Everyone has the right to freedom of peaceful assembly and to freedom of association with others, including the right to form and to join trade unions for the protection of his interests".

What is freedom of assembly and association?

The ECtHR says on its website that:

"Freedom of assembly includes public or private meetings, marches, processions, demonstrations and sit-ins. The purpose may be political, religious or spiritual, social or another purpose; no limit has been imposed on purpose, but any assembly must be peaceful. Incidental violence will not mean an assembly forfeits protection unless it had a disruptive purpose".

This is another important freedom which exists in most democratic societies where the freedom to make political comments and to have a healthy debate about controversial issues is valued. The ECtHR also says on its website that the state has a positive obligation to protect those exercising their right of peaceful assembly from violence by counter-demonstrators.

Case example

UMO Ilinden v Bulgaria 2012 involved several cases of interference by the Mayor and the police in rallies and events planned by Ilinden. Restrictions were made on the timing and organisation of its events and many were banned altogether. On occasions, the police arrested participants and seized materials from them. The ECtHR held that the measures were clearly aimed at hindering or even altogether preventing the events. It noted that rarely had explanations been given for the restrictions and even where they were it was only to say there were other events in the area.

Even if there was a risk of clashes between participants in Ilinden's rallies and counter-demonstrators, it was the task of the police to stand between the two groups and to ensure public order. This is similar to the point made in **Beatty v Gillbanks 1882**.

The ECtHR concluded that imposing bans on Ilinden's rallies was not necessary in a democratic society.

In addition to the positive obligation, the state has a negative obligation not to interfere with the right. However, the freedom is of *peaceful* assembly so the right may be subject to state interference where there may be a possible breach of the peace. The state needs to protect people from potential disorder, so activities which threaten the peace are subject to controls.

There is some overlap with **A 5** where the authorities have prevented people from going where they like. Many protests involve people getting together, or assembling, to make a political point so engage **A 10**. If these people are restrained or detained there is a possible violation of **A 5**. There is also a possible violation of **A 11** because that protects the right to get together in the first place.

Case examples

In **Austin v UK 2012**, the ECtHR held that the use of kettling as a method of crowd control would not violate **A 5** as long as it was not arbitrary, was proportionate to the purpose and was for no longer than reasonably necessary. In **Moos 2012** the use of kettling to control Climate Camp protesters was held by the HC to breach **A 5** but this was overturned on appeal. The CA stated that whether a breach of the peace was imminent was a matter for the police to decide. Both these cases involved protests which could have come within **A 10** and **A 11**.

Task 18

Look at the cases of **Austin** and **Moos** where the police had reasonable cause to fear a breach of the peace. If the police had wanted to impose conditions but the protesters claimed this would breach their **A 11** rights what do you think the court would see as relevant?

Restrictions on A 11

Article 11 (2) states:

No restrictions shall be placed on the exercise of these rights other than such as are prescribed by law and are necessary in a democratic society in the interests of national security or public safety, for the prevention of disorder or crime, for the protection of health or morals or for the protection of the rights and freedoms of others. This Article shall not prevent the imposition of lawful restrictions on the exercise of these rights by members of the armed forces, of the police or of the administration of the State.

A 11 (2) again allows measures which are *"necessary in a democratic society"* on various public interest grounds. **Austin** and **Moos** illustrate the response of the courts to what amounts to necessary. The ECtHR accepted kettling was permissible in the first case, the HC declared it was a breach in the second but the CA disagreed. **Hicks** decided kettling was an interference with **A 5** but accepted it did not breach it and made clear that much will depend on the circumstances and whether the action is proportionate to the aim it is intended to achieve.

The police can impose conditions on gatherings and marches or apply for an order to stop them altogether.

Case example

UMO Ilinden involved all the above but the ECtHR made clear that these should not be aimed at preventing protest because that is unlikely to be necessary in a democratic society. Any restriction must also be proportionate.

The restrictions on the qualified rights are similar but not identical. All three subsections allow the state or public authority to interfere with these rights where this is *"necessary in a democratic society"* and for a permitted purpose. In all three subsections these include the interests of national security or public safety, the prevention of disorder or crime, the protection of health or morals and the protection of the rights and freedoms (reputation in **A 10**) of others.

A 8 (2) adds the economic well-being of the country.

A 10 (2) adds territorial integrity, preventing the disclosure of information received in confidence and maintaining the authority and impartiality of the judiciary.

In addition, **A 8 (2)** provides that any restrictions on the right must be *"in accordance with law"*. **A 10 (2)** and **A 11 (2)** provide that any restrictions on the right must be *"prescribed by law"*.

Judges in both the domestic courts and the ECtHR have said that interference will only be justified if the action is proportionate to a legitimate aim. If interference is in order to achieve one of the stated purposes that will clearly be a legitimate aim. It will therefore be justified if proportionate. However, it must still meet the legality requirement and so be in accordance with (or prescribed by) law.

To sum up, first the court will consider whether the right has been engaged. Secondly it will consider the exceptions in paragraph 2 and whether any restrictions are:

- prescribed by or in accordance with law
- necessary in a democratic society
- for a permitted purpose (a legitimate aim)
- proportionate to the purpose (or aim)

Case examples

- In **Steinfeld and Keidan 2018** the aim was not legitimate
- In **A v the Home Department** the aim was legitimate but the restriction was not proportionate
- In **Hicks** the aim was legitimate and the restriction was proportionate
- In **Miranda** the aim was legitimate and the restriction was proportionate but was not *"prescribed by law"*

Task 19

A 8 provides that any restrictions on the right must be *"in accordance with law"*. **A 10** and **A 11** provide that any restrictions on the right must be *"prescribed by law"*. Explain these terms and how they affect restrictions on these three articles.

The margin of appreciation in all three qualified rights

The margin of appreciation given to states allows a broad discretion in the interpretation and application of the **ECHR**. It is particularly significant in these qualified rights. It not only allows the state discretion in interpretation of the right itself but also of the exceptions and justifications. Whether the margin of appreciation allows the state to avoid its obligation to protect the right may vary with time. We saw in **Goodwin** that although the state had previously had discretion in how to interpret **A 8** and to decide whether it extended to transsexuals, this was no longer the case. In earlier cases (**Rees**, **Cossey**) the ECtHR had accepted the state could exclude transsexuals, in **Goodwin** it made clear it no longer could. This shows the margin of appreciation is affected by the times and social attitudes. It is an example of the **ECHR** as a living instrument which must adapt and change. The scope of the margin of appreciation also depends on the circumstances and an important factor is whether there is common ground on the issue between the participating states. However, this is not paramount.

Example

Although the presence of common ground between states has been a factor in whether there is a margin of appreciation, in **Goodwin** the ECtHR suggested that the international trend in acceptance of transsexuals was more important than a common European approach. The court decided that the matter no longer fell within the margin of appreciation allowed to states (as had been the case in **Rees** and **Cossey**).

There are two main ways that the state may use the margin of appreciation.

- to interpret the right so that it does not cover the situation
    - as in **Rees** and **Cossey** where the margin of appreciation was used to avoid extending the right to transsexuals
    - but the margin may change over time as shown by **Goodwin**
- to interpret the exceptions under paragraph two to justify the interference with the right
    - e.g., whether interference is necessary in a democratic country and whether the purpose is to protect, e.g., security, health or morals (**UMO Ilinden**)
    - the measure must be proportionate to this aim (**Hicks**)

An example of where the UK provisions went beyond the allowed margin of appreciation is **Hirst**.

Legality, proportionality and legitimate aims

This is significant in all human rights law so there is some repetition here.

To avoid being in violation of a right, the state must justify the measure. In deciding whether it is justified, the courts will take into account whether it is proportionate in relation to a legitimate aim, as seen in **Roberts**. The purposes (national security etc.) set out in the three subsections will all be legitimate aims. The state has a margin of appreciation in interpreting these so other aims may also be legitimate. Many cases are determined on the issues of proportionality and legitimacy. These concepts are also part of English law. In all judicial review cases the court will consider whether the use of power is legitimate and proportionate in the circumstances. If not, it may be *ultra vires* (beyond the power given).

Here is a repeat of the legality requirements.

The legality requirement

A 8(2) provides that any interference with the right to respect for a private life must be *"in accordance with law"*

A 10(2) and **A 11(2)** provide that any interference with the right to freedom of expression and freedom of assembly and association must be *"prescribed by law"*

In each of these rights this is known as the legality requirement. Case law has shown that not only must there be a domestic law allowing the interference, but also that any interference conforms to the rule of law (**Gillan and Roberts**). In addition, the measure must be proportionate to a legitimate aim. This may mean that it is justified in the circumstances.

In **Steinfeld and Keidan 2018** the SC restated the four-stage test designed to establish whether interference with a qualified right was justified saying this *"is now well-established"*. There are four questions.

- is the legislative objective (legitimate aim) sufficiently important to justify limiting a fundamental right?
- are the measures which have been designed to meet it rationally connected to it?
- are they no more than are necessary to accomplish it?
- do they strike a fair balance between the rights of the individual and the interests of the community?

In that case the aim was not legitimate but the SC added that if it had been then the rational connection could be satisfied but not the rest of the test. Effectively this is the proportionality principle and the balancing of interests. The SC concluded that other measures, such as extending civil partnerships while deliberating were possible and the measures did not strike a fair balance between competing interests.

So, justification requires a rational connection to the legitimate aim and that the measures were no more than necessary to achieve the aim. This is essentially the proportionality principle and also applies to **A 5**. The SC also noted the measures must strike a fair balance between competing interests. This applies to all three qualified rights.

The following examples, decided under English laws on police powers, engaged **A 8** and **A 5** respectively. In the first case the police powers were legitimate but in the second they were not.

Case examples

In **PD v CC of Merseyside Police 2015**, a girl of fourteen had been arrested while drunk and abusive. She had a record of self-harm and for this reason her clothes were removed at the police station. She claimed breach of her rights under **A 8**. The HC recognised that under Code C of **PACE** the police had the power to seize her clothing in very limited circumstances, but one of these was to prevent her from harming herself. The court decided that although her **A 8** rights had been interfered with, this was to stop her harming herself. On balance this was not a disproportionate use of power and the aim was legitimate. The HC rejected her claim.

In **Mengesha v Commissioner of Police of the Metropolis 2013**, the HC held that the containment of people during a protest march was lawful. This was because it was in order to prevent a breach of the peace which was a legitimate aim (the prevention of disorder or crime). However, the actions of the police in insisting on photographs and private addresses being taken and retained before the claimant was allowed to leave was not lawful. This was not done in order to prevent a breach of the peace so was not *"in accordance with law"*.

In **Mengesha** the area was the subject of an authorisation under **s 60 CJPOA** but the court held this did not extend to the demand of personal details.

Evaluation pointer

A 8 uses the term *"in accordance with law"* whereas **A 10** and **11** use the term *"prescribed by law"*. This suggests these are different but there is no evidence that this is the case when looking at cases. They have both been taken to mean that any restrictions or limits on rights must be made under a valid law and comply with the rule of law. It seems an unnecessary distinction to make in the **ECHR**.

Morals: One of the legitimate purposes is measures taken *"for the protection of health or morals"*. Look at the English provisions on obscenity in the next chapter for examples.

Task 20

Any limits on these rights must be necessary and must be either in accordance with, or prescribed by, law. This means the limits must be proportionate to a legitimate aim to be achieved. Briefly explain what is meant by the term *"proportionate to a legitimate aim"* and give a case example.

More examples of the various English provisions which impact on these rights are discussed in the next chapter.

Examination pointer

Look for the overlap between **A 11**, **A 5** and **A 10** in examination questions. An example would be a group of protesters waving placards and shouting abuse. The group are free to assemble under **A 11**, although this must be peaceful. The placards would be a way to express their views so engage **A 10** and anyway the protest itself would be an expression of opinions and ideas. The state has a margin of appreciation so can restrict both these rights, e.g., in order to protect the rights of others. Shouting abuse could mean the group's rights under **A 10** give way to laws which protect others against this type of behaviour. The group members have a right to liberty under **A 5**. The state can restrict liberty *"for the purpose of bringing the person before the competent legal authority on reasonable suspicion of having committed an offence"*. If members of the group are shouting abuse in a way that constitutes an offence this will be satisfied and an arrest is unlikely to violate **A 5**.

Summary

The rights and restrictions can be explained using the case of **Miranda**. The right in question was **A 10** and the restriction on the right was the power to stop, search and remove material under the **Terrorism Act**. The CA made clear that when the situation involved journalistic material the rights under **A 10** were stronger and more was needed to justify any restriction. In order to come within the exceptions allowed under **A 10 (2)** the action must be prescribed by law. The CA held that in a case concerning journalistic material *"the availability of judicial review, after the event, cannot cure a breach of article 10"*.

The CA looked at three questions in **Miranda**. All three will be considered when deciding whether the policy or action is necessary in a democratic society. The HC had said all three were satisfied but the CA disagreed on the last point.

- Whether the restriction was allowed under national law

- - Yes, the Act was clear
- Whether the use of the power was proportionate to a legitimate aim
  - Yes, the police have expertise in assessing the risk to national security and in weighing it against competing interests. This should be taken into account when determining the proportionality of a decision taken by the police in the interests of national security
- Whether it was compatible with **A 10**
  - No, there had to be *adequate* safeguards and in the case of disclosure of journalistic material the possibility of judicial review after the event was not adequate. The safeguards were not sufficient to make the interference with the right *"prescribed by law"*.

Self-test questions

1. What is the legality requirement?
2. In **Roberts 2015** the SC said this required adherence with what in addition to a domestic law?
3. How does s **12 HRA** strengthen rights under **A 10**?
4. What legitimate aim does **A 8 (2)** add to the usual aims?
5. What was the legitimate aim in **Mengesha**?

Chapter 5 Provisions of English law which impact on Articles 8 10 and 11

The **ECHR** imposes obligations on the UK (and other states) to protect rights by virtue of national laws. Positive obligations require the state to have laws to protect the rights. Negative obligations require the state not to interfere with the rights. We have seen what the rights (and exceptions) are and what the margin of appreciation is for each of these three rights. This chapter will explore how far English domestic law meets these obligations.

Although the state must meet the obligations imposed by the **ECHR** by having laws in place to protect **ECHR** rights, it has a fair amount of discretion because as well as the margin of appreciation there are exceptions to those obligations under paragraph 2. However, any exception has to be either prescribed by or in accordance with law. The state and public authorities must therefore ensure that any interference complies with a domestic law.

Example

Using the case of **Hicks** we can say that it could involve the rights under **A 10** and **A 11** as well as **A 5**. These two rights are qualified and there are exceptions allowing the state to restrict them. The state will have to be able to show that the actions of the police complied with domestic law and met the criteria set out in paragraph two of each article.

- The restrictions were prescribed by law because the police had a right under English common law to take measures to prevent a breach of the peace
- They were for a permitted purpose as the action taken was to prevent disorder and also to protect others
- The ability to maintain public order is necessary in a democratic society and is justified as long as the measures are proportionate to a legitimate aim (or purpose)
- The measures were minor and short term so proportionate to the aim of preventing disorder and protecting the rights others
- In conclusion, the state interfered with the rights but did not breach them.

Task 21

Before looking at provisions in English law which impact on human rights look back at Human rights in the UK after the Human Rights Act 1998 in Chapter 2 to see how the **HRA** affects domestic laws and judgments.

Some provisions affect more than one article or support one and restrict another. For clarity I have separated the main provisions of English law for each article but have noted where this is the case.

When you apply the law to these three qualified rights the main points to consider are:

- how far does English law comply with the rights under these articles?
- how far is the state allowed a margin of appreciation?

Here is a reminder of the questions to ask when considering whether a measure by a public authority violates a right:

- Does the measure interfere with a right under the **ECHR**?
- Under what English law is the measure allowed?
- Does the law / measure respect the right?

- Is the measure necessary in a democratic society?
    - Is there a legitimate aim?
    - Is the measure proportionate to the aim?

If so the interference may be justified.

If not the interference may violate the right.

Provisions in English law which impact on the rights under A 8

The negative obligation on the state is not to interfere with the right to respect for a private and family life and this would include not intercepting communications or using intrusive surveillance or other invasive measures. Laws on data protection and surveillance impact on this obligation. The positive obligation is to protect the right. There is no right to privacy in English law however the state complies with this obligation by having laws against breach of confidence, misuse of private information, defamation and harassment, amongst others.

As noted in the previous chapter, this is an extremely wide-ranging right so there are a lot of English provisions which will come into play. For that reason you will need to be selective.

Examination pointer

Balancing conflicting interests: Data protection is a complex area and the law is undergoing changes so it is unlikely you will be expected to discuss this in any detail. It is a good example of the competing interests of public security and protection of privacy, though.

Misuse of private information on the other hand is important as both the ECtHR and English courts have developed this tort to protect privacy. It is also important when looking at balancing the competing rights between **A 8** and **A 10** (see next chapter).

Interception of communications, data collection and retention

We saw in Chapter 2 that the UK increased state powers on data collection and surveillance following the ECtHR ruling in **Malone**. The state argues that such powers are necessary in the interests of security. Others respond that they are not justified because they permit indiscriminate data collection and do not allow for independent scrutiny.

The challenge in **Watson 2016** was to the indiscriminate retention of personal data as allowed under the then current law the **Data Retention and Investigatory Powers Act 2014 (DRIPA)**. The CA referred the case to the Court of Justice of the European Union (CJEU) because under EU law data retention must be *"strictly necessary"* for the fighting of *"serious"* crime. In addition, access to the data must be subject to prior review by a court or an independent administrative authority. The CJEU ruled that the law was inconsistent and in **Watson & Others v Home Secretary 2018** the CA declared that the UK was in breach of **Article 7** of the **Charter of Fundamental Rights of the European Union** (commonly called the **EU Charter**). This includes all the **ECHR** rights and **A 7** is the equivalent of **A 8** of the **ECHR**. Both the **ECHR** and the **EU Charter** allow the state a margin of appreciation to avoid rights where necessary in the interests of public health or security. The data retention policy was not deemed sufficiently necessary. The issue affects many people because advances in technology have made covert surveillance and the collection of personal data simple. Following Brexit it will not be necessary to comply with **A 7** of the **EU Charter**, but the UK will still have an obligation to comply with **A 8** of the **ECHR**.

The case is an example of both types of obligation.

- The positive obligation is to protect the right to respect for a private life
  - this is not fulfilled by the English provisions as the state not only allows data collection by others, in some cases it demands it
- The negative obligation is not to interfere with the right
  - this is not fulfilled because the collection and retention is for possible use by the state

The most recent law is the **Data Protection Act 2018 (DPA 2018)**, incorporating the latest EU regulation, the **General Data Protection Regulation (GDPR) 2016**. Both came into effect in May 2018. The **DPA** got stuck in a ping-pong situation but agreement in Parliament was eventually reached and the **GDPR** has been brought into English law (although with plenty of exemptions).

Surveillance and other police powers

We looked at police powers under **PACE** in Chapter 3. The police also have powers of surveillance which are regulated by the **Police Act 1997**. This provides, e.g., that any warrant for surveillance must have authorisation from the Chief Constable or the Assistant Chief Constable.

In **Andrew v MPC 2017**, the CA held that a police inspector and her husband should receive compensation based on the illegal obtaining and retention of their mobile phone data as it breached their rights under **A 8** and was not properly authorised.

Other police powers include the taking of fingerprints, photographs and DNA samples. These can be taken and retained indefinitely where someone has been convicted of a recordable offence. In **Gaughran 2015**, a man pleaded guilty to driving with excess alcohol and then challenged the policy of retaining samples on the basis that it conflicted with **A 8**. It was an Irish case but went to the SC which noted that English law under **PACE** also allowed indefinite retention. It considered two questions:

- Was there an interference with **A 8**?
- If so, was the interference justified?

The SC noted that a blanket policy of holding such data indefinitely could conflict with **A 8**. It then considered whether the retention policy was justifiable *"and, in particular, whether it satisfies the principle of proportionality"*. The SC decided that the benefit to society of having an effective database to help in combating crime outweighed his private interest under **A 8**. The scheme was not arbitrary as it only applied to recordable offences. This indicated a *"balanced and rational judgment by the authorities"* so the policy was justified. The case is one of many examples where an English provision interferes with a right but does not violate it because it is justified under paragraph 2.

There are plenty of other English law provisions which impact on **A 8**. Most important are breach of confidence, misuse of private information, defamation and harassment. These meet the positive obligation to protect rights under **A 8** but may restrict freedom of expression under **A 10**, and freedom of assembly and association under **A 11** where an expression of opinion is involved.

Breach of confidence and misuse of private information

Breach of confidence is where information, which was communicated to a person in confidence, is used by that person without authorisation to the detriment of the person providing the information. It is often used in employment situations to prevent trade secrets being passed on and traditionally required a relationship of confidentiality. That meant that a duty of confidentiality was imposed on a person not to disclose the information. However, it has developed over the years since the **HRA**. In the following case the HL held that English law enshrined **ECHR** values and thus should prohibit the unjustified publication of private information.

Key case

In **Campbell v MGN 2004** the HL produced a test for helping to decide on the correct balance in cases of competing rights. The case started in 2001, not so long after the **HRA** came into effect, reached the HL in 2004 and the ECtHR some seven years after that. Naomi Campbell brought a case claiming breach of confidence against MGN for publishing photographs of her leaving a Narcotics Anonymous meeting and suggesting she was a drug addict. She accepted part of this was fair comment but objected to further pictures and discussion of her treatment, which she argued was a private matter. The HC held that her right to a private life under **A 8 ECHR** outweighed MGN's right to freedom of expression under **A 10** and awarded her £3,500 in damages. The CA then reversed this decision and ruled in favour of MGM and **A 10**. The case went to the HL which upheld the original decision, but by a majority of only 3-2. The HL accepted that breach of confidence extended to matters that were private rather than confidential and established a two-stage test. First, the court has to decide if there was an expectation of privacy. Second, it has to balance that expectation under **A 8** with the publisher's rights to freedom of expression under **A 10**. When the case eventually got to the ECtHR, on an application from MGN in **MGN v UK 2011**, the HL decision and reasoning was confirmed. Although there was some interference with MGN's right to freedom of expression it was justified.

Key principle: The court must decide whether there is an expectation of privacy and balance this against freedom of expression.

I made this a key case for several reasons. It went through the English courts and then to the ECtHR on a petition challenging the decision of the HL. It established a test for cases of conflict, extended the law on breach of confidence and first identified the separate tort of misuse of private information. It shows the need to balance rights under the two articles to ensure that freedom of expression is not used to harm others (this balancing exercise is discussed further in the next chapter). Finally it is an example of **s 6 HRA**. Baroness Hale said that the court, as a public authority, is required not to *"act in a way which is incompatible with a Convention right"*. She said the court is able to achieve this by *"absorbing the rights which articles 8 and 10 protect into the long-established action for breach of confidence. This involves giving a new strength and breadth to the action so that it accommodates the requirements of these articles."* This shows the effect of the **ECHR** being merged with English law to enhance the rights given. Breach of confidence was strengthened by absorbing the **ECHR** rights and further developed via **s 2** and **s 3 HRA** to produce the tort of misuse of private information.

This tort is similar to breach of confidence but relates to personal rather than secret information, e.g., details about a person's health or sex life, as information is often secret and private claims may be brought under both torts. However, there are differences.

Key cases

In **Google v Vidal-Hall 2015**, three individuals complained about Google's non-consensual use of browser-generated information which it then revealed to third parties for marketing purposes. As with the **Watson** case, this was based on **A 7** of the **EU Charter** (the equivalent of **A 8 ECHR**). The information tracked and collated by Google was private rather than confidential, so the claim would fail if it was based on breach of confidence. The CA accepted that there were two separate torts, breach of confidence and misuse of private information but added that this did not herald a new law but merely correctly labelled one that already existed.

In **NT1 and NT2 v Google 2018**, the HC also suggested the tort of misuse of private information already existed, noting that it was first identified in **Campbell 2004**.

In this case the facts were that Google's search engine provided links to third party reports regarding the two claimants' previous convictions. They asked Google to delist them and when nothing happened claimed breach of the **Data Protection Act 1998 (DPA)** and misuse of private information. The court rejected Google's argument that publication was for journalistic purposes and held that at the time of the claims **A 8** had become engaged. It had not been engaged at first because there was a public interest in the information. Publicity about what happened at trial and any conviction and sentence was part of open justice and a risk all criminals took. However, under the domestic law, the **Rehabilitation of Offenders Act 1974**, the convictions were now spent so misuse of private information became a possibility.

NT1 had been convicted for business-related activities and was currently in a similar business, so the convictions were still relevant. He also failed to prove the information was inaccurate as required by the **DPA** and his claim failed. NT2 was not in a similar business and some information was inaccurate so his claim succeeded.

Referring to **Campbell** and **Murray**, the HC held that the two-stage test from **Campbell** applies to both breach of confidence and misuse of private information. The main issue here was the first question as to whether the claimants enjoyed a reasonable expectation of privacy.

In regard to NT1 the answer was no.

In regard to NT2, the answer was yes. The circumstances had changed because he now had a young family. Continued access to information about his past convictions impacted on his family life so breached **A 8**. His claim for the information to be delisted was allowed.

Key principles: misuse of information is a tort in its own right and the **Campbell** test applies.

The **NT** case is useful in illustrating a number of issues. It demonstrates how changing circumstances can mean **A 8** becomes engaged even if not at first but that a claim may still fail on the expectation of privacy issue, as with NT1. NT2's expectation had increased as he now had a young family, so his claim succeeded. The court decided there was just enough interference to mean Google had to justify its actions. It failed to do this so an order to delist the information was made. However, no damages were awarded because although Google continued to make the information available after his request to delist it, the company had complied with the requirement under English law of taking reasonable care. Finally, the case illustrates how the law needs to develop with changing technology and how domestic law also sees the **ECHR** as a living instrument. The HC had to interpret an Act passed in 1974, many years before the internet. It also had to comply with **s 3 HRA 1998** when doing so.

Task 22

Briefly explain the right under **A 8** and whether the use of CCTV cameras in a town centre would violate this right.

Defamation

The tort of defamation protects against untrue statements which refer to a person. It allows people to claim damages for having lies printed or spoken about them to third parties or to claim an injunction to prevent further publication. However, the **Defamation Act 2013** is a negative law in that it states what is not defamation rather than what is. **S 1** provides that it is not defamation unless the untrue statement causes, or may cause, serious harm to that person's reputation. It also provides for a defence to the tort in three situations:

- **the statement is true** – it is a defence to an action for defamation for the defendant to show that the imputation conveyed by the statement complained of is substantially true
- **the statement is a matter of opinion not fact** – it is a defence to an action for defamation to show that the statement complained of was a statement of honest opinion and also the basis of the opinion was indicated, either in general or specific terms
- **the statement is reasonably believed to be a matter of public interest** – it is a defence to an action for defamation for the defendant to show that the statement complained of was, or formed part of, a statement on a matter of public interest and the defendant reasonably believed that publishing the statement complained of was in the public interest. For this defence the statement may be either of fact or opinion.

In **Reynolds 2001**, the CA held that *"Freedom of speech does not embrace freedom to make defamatory statements out of personal spite or without having a positive belief in their truth"*. This shows that a balance is needed to ensure one person's right to freedom of expression does not interfere with another's rights. With rights come obligations as we saw in Chapter 1. There is an obligation not to publish defamatory statements but freedom of expression is protected by the requirement that any harm be serious and by the defences.

Case example

In **Joseph v Spiller 2010**, D had published remarks on a website about the professionality and reliability of C and C sued in defamation. The defence then was fair comment but the case will be persuasive when interpreting the defence of honest opinion. The CA rejected the defence but the SC allowed D's appeal. For the defence of fair comment to succeed the writer had to be expressing an honest opinion on a matter of public interest. The SC added that the facts must be true and the comment must indicate, at least in general terms, the facts on which it is based. This is how the defence of honest opinion is defined in the 2013 Act.

In **Joseph v Spiller** the SC referred to judgments of the ECtHR and held that there was little scope under **A 10 (2)** for restrictions on political speech or questions of public interest. The SC thought these principles to be generally consistent with the English law of defamation. That is still likely to be the case. The **Defamation Act 2013** explicitly allows a defence for matters of public interest and in this case the statement can be of either fact or opinion. One difference is that the old defence was *"fair"* comment and this excluded statements motivated by malice. There is no such requirement in the later law. The defences ensure that the law protects **A 10** rights while prohibiting statements that may seriously harm a person's reputation.

Harassment

The **Protection from Harassment Act 1997** protects people from situations like stalking, the receipt of nuisance telephone calls or intrusive media attention which causes alarm or distress.

Cases like **Ireland & Burstow 1997** would come under this Act now. **S 1** allows for a civil claim in tort (usually for an injunction) but **s 2** makes such behaviour a criminal offence as well. **S 1** prohibits *"a course of conduct"* (it has to happen on more than one occasion) which may cause harassment. Harassment includes words as well as conduct.

Harassment is not fully defined in the **Act** but includes causing alarm or distress such that a reasonable person would regard as harassment. Harassment law protects **A 8** rights but restricts freedom of expression under **A 10**. As with defamation, the courts are reluctant to allow the law to restrict on rights under **A 10**. In **Trimingham v Associated Newspapers 2012**, the judge said that *"harassment must not be given an interpretation which restricts the right to freedom of expression"* and refused a claim by a woman against a newspaper which had published several articles about an affair between her and an MP.

Harassment could easily occur during a protest march or assembly so could also engage **A 11** (though it must happen on more than one occasion).

Under **s 1 (3)** there is a defence where the course of conduct was pursued for the purpose of preventing or detecting a crime, to comply with legal requirements or that in the particular circumstances the course of conduct was reasonable. In **Trimingham**, the judge made clear that the principle that the law should not be interpreted so as to restrict freedom of expression also applied when considering what a reasonable person would think amounted to harassment and when considering whether the conduct was reasonable in the circumstances for the defence to succeed.

The defence is unlikely to apply to private citizens. In **Howlett v Holding 2006**, D had been using an aircraft to drop leaflets and to fly banners referring to C, and had put her under secret surveillance because he believed she was committing benefit fraud. This amounted to harassment. An injunction was granted to prevent him from carrying out any surveillance or flying the aircraft with banners referring to her. He argued that the conduct causing the harassment was in order to prevent and detect a crime. The court interpreted **s 1 (3)** as intended to apply only to law enforcement agencies, not to private citizens.

Defamation relates to reputation, harassment to well-being and both may overlap with breach of confidence and misuse of private information. Claims in all cases would usually be for an injunction to prevent the action or further disclosure. Damages will rarely suffice as monetary compensation cannot repair damage to reputation or prevent breach or harassment. An injunction is usually only granted following a successful court action. However, with personal or private information C may want to prevent it getting out in the first place. This means applying for an interim injunction before the full trial. This is an injunction to prevent publication until the full hearing where it will be confirmed if the action succeeds or dismissed if it fails.

NT v Google showed the overlap between data protection, defamation and misuse of private information. The tort of defamation also involves passing on information and would apply where information referring to C was given to a third party was false. Google had argued that the claims were an attempt to get round the stricter defamation law and so an abuse of process. The HC held that the torts served a different purpose but had similarities so there was no abuse.

Task 23

Des repeatedly made silent telephone calls, accompanied by heavy breathing, to three women. The women suffered psychiatric illness. Advise them whether they can claim damages for interference with their **A 8** rights.

Other provisions

We have seen that human rights law has led to a liberalisation of UK laws on sexual activities. The ruling in **Goodwin v UK 2002** that the UK law which prevented transsexuals from marrying breached **A 8** led to the **Gender Recognition Act 2004**. English law now recognises the acquired gender rather than the gender at birth and complies with **A 8**.

The state has a duty to protect and promote private life and **A 8** has been the focus of many assisted dying cases (it is wider than the right to life under **A 2**). Both the domestic courts and the ECtHR have suggested that English law as it stands may interfere with a person's rights under **A 8**. Assisting a suicide remains illegal under **s 2** of the **Suicide Act 1961** and the **Act** further allows the DPP discretion as to when to prosecute. The DPP issued a code giving guidelines on when to prosecute which included whether it was in the public interest to do so.

In **Pretty v UK 2002** the HL held that **A 8** protected personal autonomy while a person was alive but did not extend to a right to choose when or how to die. The ECtHR did not agree and considered there was a possible interference with her **A 8** right because she was prevented by English law from making an informed choice. However, it accepted the law was necessary in a democratic society. In **R (on the application of Purdy) v DPP 2009** the HL held that the guidelines on when to prosecute a family member who assists in a suicide were insufficiently clear. Mrs Purdy was unable to make an informed choice as to whether or not to ask her husband to help her travel abroad. She did not want to expose him to the risk of being prosecuted but the guidelines did not state what factors will be taken into consideration in deciding whether or not it is in the public interest to prosecute those who give such assistance. The important point in this case is that the HL disagreed with its own previous decision in **Pretty** and decided that **A 8** was engaged in such cases. The HL stated that **A 8** entitled her to be provided with guidance from the DPP as to how he would exercise his discretion under the Act so had been breached. The court noted that the DPP's code was not offence-specific and made an order that it should be clarified. In particular, it should identify the facts and circumstances which the DPP will take into account in deciding whether to prosecute in a case like Ms Purdy's. The code was amended, so the law moved on a little, but many cases continue to be brought on this issue.

One example is **Conway 2017**. In this case the man had fewer than six months to live. The CA recognised the English law could be incompatible with his **A 8** rights and allowed a judicial review. However, the HC decided the **Suicide Act** did not violate **A 8** because the law was necessary and justified to protect the weak and vulnerable.

Balancing conflicting interests: All three rights in this chapter require a balancing act to be performed, although the greatest conflict is between **A 8** and **A 10** as seen in **Campbell**. There are many other cases between celebrities wanting some privacy and those who would publish stories about them, so I have devoted a section to the balancing act in the next chapter.

Summary of provisions that impact on A 8

Diagram: Central node "Article 8 the right to respect for a private and family life" surrounded by:
- A 8 (2) provisions
- Anti-terrorism laws
- Data retention legislation
- Investigatory powers legislation
- Defamation Act 2013
- Breach of confidence
- Misuse of private information
- Protection from Harassment Act 1997
- Breach of the peace

Provisions in English law which impact on the rights under A 10

The positive obligation on the state is to protect the right to freedom of expression. Laws that comply with this duty include freedom of information and the defences to defamation seen above. The obligation would also require ensuring access to justice and so is undermined by the severe cuts to legal aid and advice under **LASPO**. The negative obligation is not to interfere with freedom of expression. English law has long respected the need for freedom of the press and other media and limited any attempt at regulation. At one time the government could issue a notice to suppress newspapers publishing information (called a 'D notice') but since 2015 this has been a voluntary code of practice overseen by the Defence and Security Media Advisory Committee, which is independent of government.

However, as with the other qualified rights the state may restrict freedom of expression for a number of reasons. As well as breach of confidence and misuse of private information, the **Contempt of Court Act**, the **Official Secrets Act**, blasphemy, obscenity, harassment and racial hatred laws all have an impact along with other laws imposing regulation or censorship. As we saw earlier protection of **A 8** rights will often restrict **A 10** and **A 11** rights, showing the need to achieve a balance.

Freedom of Information and data protection

Freedom of expression involves both the freedom to communicate information and the freedom to receive it (*to receive and impart information*). **A 10** is therefore constrained not only by regulations which prevent communication or publication, but also by restrictions on access to information. The **Freedom of Information Act (FOIA) 2000** allows people access to information held by any organisation that exercises functions of a public nature, not just public authorities. This supports **A 10** as information on which to base a statement or expression is often needed before this right can be relied on. The **FOIA** therefore goes some way to improving access to information but has its limits as there are a large number of exemptions.

Case examples

In **Sugar v BBC 2012**, the applicant wanted access to a report prepared by the BBC relating to its coverage of the Middle East conflict. The HL held this was exempt under the **FOIA** because it was partly prepared for journalistic purposes. The HL made clear there was a need to balance the right to freedom of information, i.e., to receive material, with the need to protect the rights of journalists whose activities could be affected by the knowledge that they may have to disclose material. The latter rights prevailed.

In **Kennedy v Charity Commission 2014**, a journalist wanted access to documents held by the Charity Commission in relation to an enquiry it had made. He was refused a request under the **FOIA** by the Commission which relied on **s 32 FOIA** providing for an exemption in the case of documents relating to an enquiry. The applicant argued that the exemption should finish with the enquiry and if not that it breached his rights under **A 10**.

The SC held it could not interpret the provision under **s 3 HRA** to comply with **A 10** because the **FOIA** was clear. The effect of the exemption was to put the matter outside the scope of the **FOIA**. The SC also refused to issue a declaration of incompatibility under **s 4** and held that ECtHR case law had made clear that **A 10** creates no general right to freedom of information.

This was a majority judgment, the minority thought that there was an interference with his **A 10** rights and that **s 3** could be used to interpret the **FOIA** to avoid this (by interpreting the exemption to apply up to the end of the enquiry and no further).

The majority did, however, suggest that English common law could provide a remedy because under this law the courts had the power to order the disclosure of material if it was in the public interest. If that was the case then there was no breach of **A 10** because the English law complied.

Kennedy shows the effect of the English law provisions on **ECHR** rights. The Charity Commission is a public authority so subject to judicial review (of its decision to refuse disclosure). The court has the right in judicial review proceedings to order disclosure if the review succeeds. Thus, he had a remedy under English law so the state had met its positive obligations under the **ECHR** to have a domestic law in place to protect his rights.

Sugar shows competing interests within the same Article. The rights of the media to freedom of expression (to communicate information) prevailed over the individual's right to freedom of expression (to receive information).

The **DPA 2018** also provides for access to information. It confers rights on individuals to obtain information about the processing of personal data and to require inaccurate personal data to be rectified. Processing includes collection and retention so goes some way to addressing the indiscriminate retention of data issue. It also confines retention to serious crime. However, the **GDPR** allows states a margin of appreciation in the same way as the **ECHR** does, and sets out a large number of legitimate aims. The **DPA** takes full advantage of these and adds to them. The many exemptions will impact on both **A 8** and **A 10**.

In March 2018, the New Law Journal voiced the concern of several lawyers that the new law posed new dangers. It provides for an *"immigration-control exemption"* which allows the Home Office to deny people access to information about their immigration status and other personal data. Many challenges to Home Office decisions on immigration, detention and deportation will become more difficult because people will be denied access to the information on which any decision is based. Inability to challenge a decision has a direct impact on freedom of expression. Lawyers and human rights groups called for the exemption to be removed. However, despite the fact that it is not one of the legitimate aims listed in the **GDPR** it remains. The **DPA** also imposes a duty on lawyers to give the Information Commissioner's Office access to legally privileged material *"thus undermining the centuries-old right to confidential legal advice"*. This could lead to a claim for breach of confidence.

Defamation, breach of confidence, contempt of court, official secrets and trespass

We looked at defamation and breach of confidence with **A 8**. These are specifically permitted under **A 10 (2)** which allows laws *"for the protection of the reputation or rights of others, for preventing the disclosure of information received in confidence"*.

Task 24

> The tort of defamation protects against untrue statements referring to a person which may cause serious harm to that person's reputation. Briefly explain what breach of confidence and misuse of private information protect against and identify a case which developed each of these torts.

The **Official Secrets Act 1989** restricts the passing on of information gained through working for the state. All civil servants must sign this.

Case example

> In **Ponting 1985**, a civil servant leaked confidential documents about the sinking of the Argentinian ship General Belgrano by the British during the Falklands War. He was prosecuted under the **Official Secrets Act 1911** (now **1989**).

The **Contempt of Court Act 1981** restricts publication of matters in court during a case which may prejudice the trial. It also covers disobeying a court order.

The 'Spycatcher affair' was a famous English case involving both **Acts** as well as freedom of expression and breach of confidence. In 1985, a former MI5 officer (Peter Wright) wrote a book called Spycatcher containing details about the intelligence services that the government did not want made public. He had signed the **Official Secrets Act** so was prohibited from giving away such secrets. The book was banned in England despite being widely available elsewhere, including Scotland. Several newspapers were involved in court cases because they printed extracts from the book. In 1986 the Attorney-General was granted interim injunctions against the Observer and Guardian based on breach of confidence and these were upheld by the CA and HL. Later cases against the Independent and several other newspapers came under the **Contempt of Court Act** because they had published extracts after the court injunctions had been granted and the injunctions were held to be binding on all newspapers. There was widespread public criticism of the judicial decisions supporting the ban. After three years of cases the HL ruled that as the book was so widely available it was no longer giving away secrets. In a 1991 case brought by the Observer the ECtHR ruled the ban breached **A 10**. The case shows how the UK used the margin of appreciation too widely and restricted the right to freedom of expression. It also shows how any expectation of privacy can change over time so that rights under **A 8** may give way to rights under **A 10**.

Case example

Following the upholding of the ban in the English courts the newspapers petitioned the commission. In **Observer and Guardian v UK 1991** the ECtHR considered whether the action was necessary in a democratic society and whether the UK had a legitimate aim in interfering with the rights under **A 10**. The answer to this was yes, but not any longer. The injunctions had originally been imposed to preserve the confidentiality of what were at the time unpublished allegations. That confidentiality had been destroyed by the publication of the book. The earlier restrictions on the right were for a legitimate aim, but that was no longer the case.

Trespass can be both to the person and a place. In **Kaye v Robertson 1990** (see Chapter 2), the actor wanted to prevent publication of a supposed interview and photographs taken of him in hospital following brain surgery. The CA ruled out trespass both to the place and the person because he was not the legal occupier of the hospital room and he was not touched.

Obscenity, racial hatred, censorship and blasphemy

Morals: All these restrictions on **A 10** may be justified as necessary to protect the rights of others or to protect morality.

In **Gillberg v Sweden** the ECtHR made clear **A 10** should be widely construed in a democratic society when it said it applied not only to inoffensive information and ideas "*but also to those that offend, shock or disturb*". However, the court added "*subject to paragraph two*". This means a state is allowed to have laws to restrict such material if necessary in a democratic society to protect, e.g., morality.

The **Obscene Publications Act 1959** restricts the publication of material to be read or looked at which is likely to deprave and corrupt. Under **s 1** publication includes distribution, circulation, selling, hiring and even giving the material away. In the case of recorded material it includes showing, projecting or transmitting the material. The law restricts **A 10** but also supports it because there is a defence under **s 4** if, in the interests of ballet, drama, opera or other art, learning or literature, publication is justified as being for the public good. Under common law the offence of outraging public decency is similar but requires a public act in the presence of at least two people.

Case example

In **Gibson and another 1991**, a conviction of outraging public decency at common law was upheld on appeal. D ran an art gallery and displayed a model's head with an earring made out of a freeze-dried human foetus. He argued that the common law offence no longer applied but the CA held that the **Obscene Publications Act 1959** did not preclude such an action.

Now that **s 3 HRA** requires the courts to interpret English law to comply with **A 10** the prosecution could fail. However, the state would argue the law was necessary for the protection of morals.

The **Racial and Religious Hatred Act 2006**, prohibits the incitement of hatred due to someone's race or religion and therefore prevents freedom of expression in such circumstances. Further, the **Criminal Justice and Immigration Act 2008** prohibits possession of extreme pornographic images. This would include photographs and videos, although works with a classified certificate are excluded. The **Communications Act 2003** also restricts **A 10**. **S 127** makes it a criminal offence to use a public electronic communications network to send a message that is *"grossly offensive"*. There is no specific law regulating social media posts but this section has been used to restrict abusive comments on Twitter and Facebook posts.

Much of this area links to law and technology because as technology becomes more sophisticated it is easier for the state to spy on people. The internet and social media has also had an impact on human rights because it easier to circulate information.

Case example

In **Viscount St Davids 2017**, an aristocrat had posted abusive and racist material on Facebook and was charged under the **Communications Act 2003**. His attempt to rely on **A 10** failed. The UK judge stated that **A 10** *"is a proportionate freedom and this does not allow you to send menacing posts in the way I find you have"*.

Local councils also have powers to pass by-laws banning material that (in their opinion) is blasphemous, indecent or otherwise morally offensive. An example is the Monty Python film *"The Life of Brian"* which some councils banned, but others allowed. If you wanted to see it you could just get on a bus! All these laws restrict what can be printed or broadcast so engage **A 10**.

Task 25

What possible restrictions on **A 10** could apply to the following?

- An article about someone
- Giving out information received at work
- A protest against government policy

A 10 states that *"This Article shall not prevent States from requiring the licensing of broadcasting, television or cinema enterprises."* In English law, the issue of a licence is subject to meeting required standards. Both the press and broadcasting have Standards Commissions and the film industry is subject to the British Board of Censors. Following the Leveson Report on press ethics and culture in 2012, the Independent Press Standards Organisation (IPSO) and the Press Recognition Panel were established in 2014. The first aims to protect individual rights and uphold high standards of journalism while at the same time helping to maintain freedom of expression. The latter was set up by royal charter to ensure that regulators of the UK press are independent, properly funded and able to protect the public.

Evaluation pointer

In his report Lord Leveson noted that politicians and the press had been too close and that press behaviour had, at times, been *"outrageous"*. A similar point was made by the judge in **Kaye**, showing little had changed. Perhaps now there will be a better balance between protection of individual rights and freedom of the press.

There has been much debate about the need to regulate social media companies such as Facebook and Google but so far no laws. With cyber-bullying and online abuse becoming a real concern it is likely to happen at some point. Currently the options are to use laws aimed at other types of publication such as defamation or misuse of private information. The **Communications Act** could be used to prosecute someone, as in **Viscount St Davids**.

Police powers and breach of the peace

We have looked at breach of the peace with **A 5**. Here is an example under **A 10**.

Case example

In **Hashman and Harrup v UK 2000**, protesters against fox hunting had tried to disrupt a hunt by blowing horns and being disruptive. They were found to have breached the peace and were given a court order to *"be of good behaviour"*. They argued that the UK was in breach of **A 10** in limiting their freedom of expression. The ECtHR held that the court order was not sufficiently precise and certain to comply with the requirement under **A 10 (2)** that any limitations on freedom of expression be *"prescribed by law"*.

Examination pointer

When applying the law you will need to explain the right and any restrictions on it and then consider whether there is a provision of English law which covers the situation. Discuss whether the provision is necessary and whether it was justified (it was made to achieve a legitimate aim and was proportionate to that aim). Note that the courts will abide by **s 2** and **s 3 HRA** and if possible ensure the rights are protected by the national provisions. If that is not possible a declaration may be made under **s 4 HRA** that it is incompatible with the **ECHR**.

Again, note the overlap between the rights. In **Beghal** the domestic court ruled the stopping of someone at an airport had not breached **A 5**. In **Miranda**, in similar circumstances, the right came under **A 10** because it related to journalistic material.

Let us take the case of **Kaye** as an example to see how some of the English laws would apply.

Example

In **Kaye v Robertson 1990** (see Chapter 2), an actor brought an action in several torts in an attempt to prevent publication of a supposed interview and photographs taken of him in hospital following brain surgery. The CA ruled out trespass both to the place and the person because he was not the legal occupier of the hospital room and he was not touched. Defamation law required that society would think less of the person and this was not the case. The **2013 Act** requires that serious harm is caused to a person's reputation so it would still not apply. The only possibility was malicious falsehood. The CA explained the ingredients of this tort as publication of *"words which are false"* and *"published maliciously"*. Special damage must also be suffered because of the publication in order to claim damages. An injunction could be used to prevent the newspaper falsely claiming that he had consented. However, despite the CA stating that the journalist had been irresponsible and had invaded the actor's privacy it concluded that publication of the article was not against the UK law. No remedy was available.

Breach of confidence under the common law was not claimed but many later claims under **A 8** have been based on this, e.g., **Campbell**. The tort protects information seen as private and was the nearest to a 'privacy' law the UK had before the **HRA** came into force. Since then national courts are required to take into account decisions of the ECtHR and the tort has increased in potential and developed into a tort of misuse of information (see **Google v Vidal-Hall**). This is based on whether there is a reasonable expectation of privacy rather than whether there is a relationship of confidence between the parties. A claim *could* have succeeded in **Kaye** based on breach of confidence, now a claim based on misuse of private information would almost certainly succeed because personal information about his health was disclosed.

We saw in **Miranda** that although the CA held the stop to be lawful because it was not disproportionate (to the aim of preventing classified material reaching the public domain and endangering security), it issued a declaration of incompatibility because there were inadequate safeguards against the arbitrary exercise of the power. The stop was related to journalistic material and was not *"prescribed by law"* as required by **A 10 (2).** The powers used were lawful under English law but were not compatible with the **ECHR.**

Task 26

Why did the case of **Miranda** come under **A 10** but in similar circumstances the case of **Beghal** came under **A 5**?

Summary of provisions that impact on A 10

- A 10 (2) provisions
- Freedom of Information Act 2000
- Malicious falsehood
- Defamation Act 2013
- Blasphemy laws
- Public Order Act 1986
- Official Secrets Act 1989
- Contempt of Court Act 1981
- Communications Act 2003
- Racial and Religious Hatred Act 2006
- Plus Article 8 provisions

Article 10 the right to freedom of expression

Provisions in English law which impact on the rights under A 11

The freedom to meet with others and to protest has long been a tradition in English law, as it is in most democratic states. In **Beatty v Gillbanks 1882**, the court ruled that people had the right to march peacefully and lawfully even though another group opposed them and thus threatened trouble. This illustrates the state meeting its positive obligation to protect the rights under **A 10** to meet freely and to protest by way of demonstrations or processions. As Lord Hope said in **Austin**, *"one of the features of a vigorous and healthy democracy is that people are allowed to go out onto the streets and demonstrate"*. It is possible that in such circumstances the state should not only allow the first group to march but also should take positive action to prevent the other group from interfering.

As with most civil liberties under English law, these *"rights"* are residual freedoms not rights. They are only allowed in so far as there is no law restricting them. Domestic law on the right to assemble and meet freely illustrates this. People are allowed to get together and march together and discuss matters together only subject to the proviso that there is not a law preventing this behaviour. There are, however, many such laws and extensive police powers as we saw with **A 5**. Many of these may breach the negative obligation not to interfere with the right. If so the state will argue they are necessary to protect the public. The courts will have to balance the rights of the public against those of the individual and decide if the measure is justified.

Obstruction of the highway

This can be both a tort (nuisance) and a crime under the **Highways Act 1980**. **S 137** provides that it is an offence *"in any way"* to wilfully obstruct the free passage along a highway. The police can take preventative measures which could conflict with **A 11** (and possibly **A 5**). However, the courts have added an element of unreasonableness. In **DPP v Jones and Lloyd 1999**, the HL held that a group protesting against the fencing at Stonehenge had the right to assembly *"so long as such assembly does not* unreasonably *obstruct the highway"*. The addition of unreasonableness is less restrictive than **s 137** so supports **A 11** rights and better meets the state's obligation to protect them.

Breach of the peace

A 11 includes the word *"peaceful"*. The state would therefore be allowed to restrict the right where the assembly is not peaceful or where there is evidence it may become violent. We saw with **A 5** that the police may act to prevent a breach of the peace as defined in **Howell 1981**. This includes harm to people or property or the threat of it. So any violence or threat of it during a meeting or procession will allow the state (usually the police) to take preventative action. Whether action taken to prevent a breach of the peace will be seen as necessary will depend on the circumstances. To justify interference the action must be proportionate to the aim it is intended to achieve. We saw this in **Austin** and **Moos** with **A 5**.

The Public Order Act 1986 (POA)

The main restrictions on **A 11** come under **s 11** to **s 14**.

Section	What it controls	What is required
S 11	Processions	Written notice must be given to the police 6 days in advance unless it is not reasonably practicable. This gives details of the march and must include the date, time and route and the name and address of the organiser.
S 12	Processions	If a senior police officer reasonably believes from these details that the procession may result in serious public disorder, serious damage to property or serious disruption to the life of the community, or if the purpose is to intimidate others, conditions may be imposed.
S 13	Processions	If a senior police officer reasonably believes that the powers under **s 12** will not be sufficient to prevent serious public disorder, an application can be made to the local authority. The council can impose a blanket ban on all processions in the area for up to 3 months. In London the order can be made by the Commissioner of Police. In both cases the approval of the Secretary of State is required.
S 14	Static assemblies	This provides the same powers as **s 12** but for assemblies not processions, and the "reasonable belief" is based on the time, place and circumstances. **S 14 (a)** allows for an application to prohibit assemblies in a similar way to **s 13** for processions but only where they are trespassing. **S 14 (c)** includes the power to prevent people from going to an assembly if a prohibition order is in place. **S 14 (b)** makes it an offence to organise or take part in such an assembly.

We saw that **s 60 CJPOA** gives a senior police officer power to authorise stop and search in anticipation of violence. This Act also impacts on **A 11**. It gives the police power to make people leave the land they are on and to break up gatherings of more than 20 where loud music is played which could *"seriously distress"* the locals. The latter is used to restrict the movement of those attending or preparing to attend raves. In England and Wales the number was reduced from 100 by the **Anti-social Behaviour Act 2003**. It is still 100 in Scotland. The following case exemplifies most of these powers as the HL went through them in some detail. A summary follows the facts.

Case example

In **R (on the application of Laporte) v CC of Gloucestershire 2006**, three coaches transporting anti-war protesters were stopped at a lay-by on their way from London to Fairford RAF base. The police had evidence of items being carried that could create a breach of the peace. The search revealed items such as hard hats, masks and shields. A senior police officer ordered that the coaches return to London under police escort. The coaches were not allowed to stop and no-one could get off, leading to some discomfort. The claimant bought a judicial review case to question the legality of the police actions based on freedom of expression (**A 10**) and assembly (**A 11**). The HL held that the police action was not unlawful as far as stopping the coaches going on to the airbase because a breach of the peace was feared. This was a legitimate aim. However, the order to return was not proportionate so could not be justified. There was no longer a reason to fear a breach of the peace so both **A 10** and **A 11** rights had been breached.

Although the police had relied on powers to prevent a breach of the peace rather than the **POA**, the judgment is useful as the HL not only explained both statutory and common law public order powers but also considered whether the actions were proportionate to a legitimate aim and so justified under **A 10 (2)**. Although any discussion of the **POA** provisions would be *obiter dicta* and not binding (because the final decision was based on breach of the peace powers) they will be highly persuasive as the case was in the HL.

Summary of the points discussed:

S 11 POA: the protestors had given notice of the procession as required

S 12 POA: ordering the coaches to return to London would be within the powers under **s 12** if the police feared serious public disorder and their actions were proportionate to the legitimate aim of avoiding this

S 13 POA: the HL noted that the Chief Constable had considered seeking an order prohibiting all processions in the Fairford area for a period, but had decided not to do so

S 14 POA: during the stop at the lay-by the procession became an assembly. The HL noted that a senior police officer who reasonably believed either of the matters set out in **s 12** could impose conditions on a public assembly and that the remainder of **s 14** follows **s 12**. However, the HL made clear that there was no power comparable with **s 13**, to prohibit the holding of a public assembly not involving a trespass. This was not the case here

S 60 CJPOA: the HL noted the Chief Constable had used the power given in **s 60** to authorise searches for weapons and this included the power to search both people and vehicles

Breach of the peace: the HL noted that despite these legislative powers the common law still applied and referred to the definition in **Howell**

Restrictions: the HL noted that neither the **A 10** nor the **A 11** right is absolute and *"the exercise of these rights may be restricted if the restriction is prescribed by law, necessary in a democratic society and directed to any one of a number of specified ends"*

Justification: the HL confirmed that in general terms **s 12** and **s 13 POA** complied with the **ECHR**. The police had acted in the interests of national security, to prevent disorder and to protect the rights of others, all of which were legitimate aims under **A 10 (2)**. However, on the facts the actions were not proportionate. The passengers were *"virtually prisoners"* and the police had not shown that there were no less intrusive measures that could have been taken, so the action was not justified

The remedy: The HL granted the claimant a declaration that the police actions were unlawful because they were not prescribed by law and were disproportionate. As regards damages the case was returned to the HC for these to be assessed

A 5: A further point is that **A 5** was also an issue, although not discussed in detail in the appeals. The court of first instance had found a breach of **A 5** because the coaches were not allowed to stop and no-one could get off. Keeping people contained for two and a half hours was not a proportionate action so was not a justified interference with the right to liberty.

A protest march or an assembly is a way of expressing opinions so police powers under the **POA** and/or to prevent a breach of the peace may engage both **A 10** and **A 11**.

Additional examples of the overlap include blasphemy laws, harassment and other constraints on freedom of expression. All could be relevant to an assembly or procession involving expressions of some kind so restrict both **A 10** and **A 11** while protecting the **A 8** rights of those at the receiving end of any abuse or harassment.

Task 27 application practice

Animal rights activists are protesting outside a town centre shop that sells fur coats. They stop customers going in and hand them leaflets showing shocking pictures of animal's being trapped and killed. Although they are peaceful there are soon hundreds of protesters spilling into the street. The police arrive and attempt to disperse the protesters and arrest the first three people they see. Explain to these people what their rights are under the **ECHR** and whether they can take any action against the police.

Summary of provisions that impact on A 11

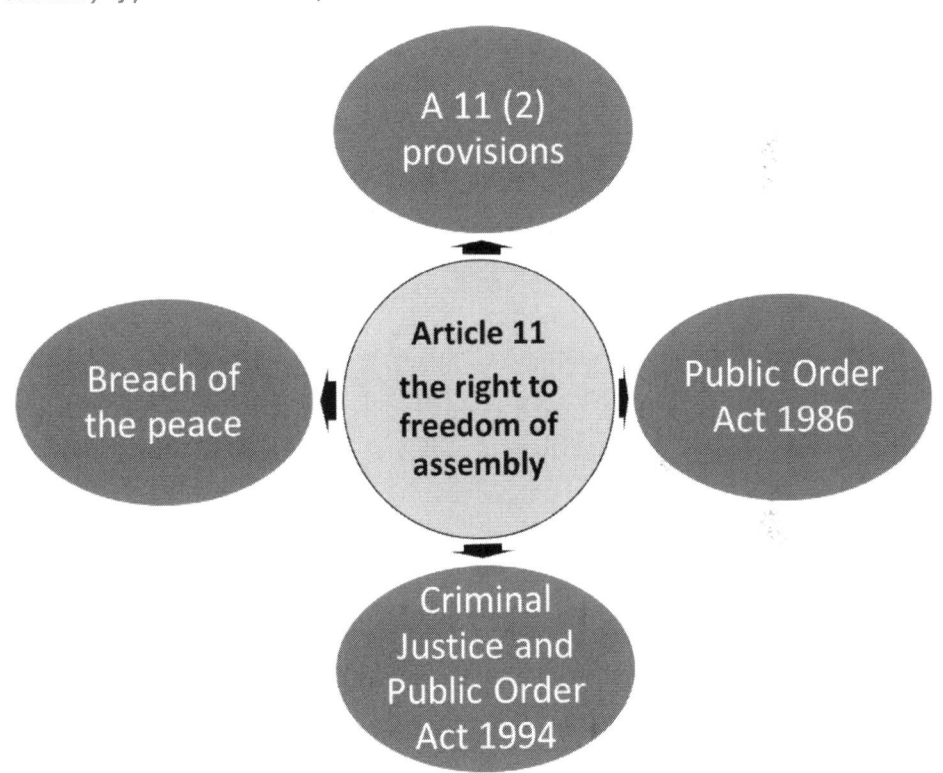

- A 11 (2) provisions
- Breach of the peace
- Public Order Act 1986
- Criminal Justice and Public Order Act 1994

Central: Article 11 the right to freedom of assembly

Self-test questions

1. In which case was the retention of personal samples justified and why?
2. **A 10 (2)** allows laws "for the protection of the reputation or rights of others, for preventing the disclosure of information received in confidence". Name two English laws which come within this.
3. Why would cuts to legal aid and advice under **LASPO** undermine freedom of expression?

4. In the Spycatcher case why did the courts decide the injunction should be lifted after so many years of banning the book?

5. In which case did the judge say that "harassment must not be given an interpretation which restricts the right to freedom of expression"

6. What restriction on police powers to prohibit assemblies under *s 14 POA* does not apply to processions under *s 13*?

Chapter 6 Balancing the rights and enforcement

Balancing conflicting interests: You have seen a few examples of balancing competing interests as all human rights cases involve a conflict either between the state and the individual or, as is the case with the competing rights under **A 8** and **A 10**, between individuals. This chapter will explore more case examples on these two articles.

I have put balancing the rights together with enforcement in order to achieve a balance myself (in my case chapter lengths). You can treat them separately but note that there is a great deal of interplay and no clear dividing line not only between these rights and restrictions, but also between the balancing acts, enforcement and remedies.

Examination pointer

Human rights law is useful when illustrating balancing competing interests as most rights under the **ECHR** (private interests) will conflict with the rights of the state, e.g., on measures to maintain order and protect society (public interests). The competing freedoms under the **ECHR** may also have to be balanced against each other. These competing interests may be between two private interests (e.g., an individual celebrity and a newspaper publisher) or between public interest and private interests (e.g., society as a whole, whose members wish to know about those in the public eye, and the individuals concerned).

Balancing the rights

The most obvious conflict arises in cases of privacy vs. freedom of expression. The conflict is not only between these two rights but also between private and public interests. There have been a great many cases involving people in the public eye who have relied on **A 8** to try to prevent publication of photographs or data about their private lives (the private interest). The media has relied on **A 10** to argue in favour of publication of such material and also argued it is in the public interest.

The following examples are just a few from the many cases where the rights conflicted. In **Kaye** (see Chapter 2), despite stating that the journalist had been grossly irresponsible and had invaded the actor's privacy, the CA held that this was not against the UK law. Cases since the **HRA** have met with greater success because judges must take into account decisions of the ECtHR (**s 2**) and interpret domestic law to comply with the **ECHR** if possible (**s 3**).

In **Campbell** (see previous chapter) the balance tipped in favour of her **A 8** rights. In **Ferdinand v MGN Ltd 2011** the balance tipped the other way. Rio Ferdinand tried to prevent publication of an article alleging that he had had an affair. In several articles and in his autobiography he had given the impression that he was a family man and had given up "*playing around*". He was also the England football captain, so his conduct was of public interest. The HC held that the balance of interest lay in protecting the publisher's freedom of expression over the footballer's right to privacy. The next case was heard in the ECtHR; all the following examples were decided in the English courts (remember that under **s 2 HRA** national courts must take into account decisions of the ECtHR.). The fact that they were all decided without recourse to the ECtHR shows the effect of the **HRA**.

In **Von Hannover** (see Chapter 4), the ECtHR held that the right to press freedom will outweigh privacy concerns where, for example, facts are reported about politicians in the exercise of their functions. Such reporting was deemed by the ECtHR to be an example of the press exercising its vital role as "*watchdog*" in a democratic society.

The ECtHR restated the balance that should be made between **A 8** and **A 10** in respect of the publication of photographs. The court set down five things to take into consideration:

- the contribution made by the material to the debate of general interest
- how well known the person was and the subject of the report
- the prior conduct of the individual concerned
- the content, form and consequences of publication
- the circumstances in which the photo was taken

The ECtHR held that Germany had achieved a fair balance between the two rights. The court had granted an injunction against some photographs being printed and had taken the correct matters into account in allowing publication of others. In particular, the court had considered the important question of whether the photographs had contributed to a debate of general public interest and was correct in deciding there was a genuine public interest in the princess and her family.

In **A v B 2000**, a footballer obtained an injunction to suppress publication of details of his extra-marital affairs but the CA reversed the decision. Although it dismissed the injunction, the CA suggested that such relationships might require the protection of the law, and issued guidelines on how to decide this. These illustrate the matters the courts will take into consideration when trying to balance **A 8** and **A 10** interests. They include the type of relationship involved, how the information was obtained, how much of a public figure the person was and/or how much publicity was sought by that person. In this case the CA concluded an injunction would be *"an unjustified interference with the freedom of the press"*. The balance fell in favour of the **A 10** right to freedom of expression.

The two-stage test from **Campbell** was approved in **Weller v Associated Newspapers 2015** by the CA, which made clear that if the case involved a child, age was a relevant factor. Other factors included the nature and purpose of the intrusion. The court made clear that a child's **A 8** rights did not trump **A 10** rights but *"they must be given considerable weight"*. The pictures were of Paul Weller (former member of the Style Council) and his children. Although he was a public figure and the pictures were taken in a public place, it was a private family outing. This tipped the balance in favour of the private interests of the children under **A 8**. This is similar to **Murray v Express Newspapers 2008** in the table in Chapter 1.

Evaluation pointer

There is a direct and obvious conflict between these two articles. This arguably makes the law unclear and also takes up a lot of court time in the attempt to balance the interests and resolve the conflict.

Task 28

Compare the cases of **Campbell** and **Ferdinand**. Explain why the decisions were different and where the balance of the competing interests lay in each case.

In **V v Associated Newspapers and others 2016**, the HC had to balance a family's **A 8** interests with the media's **A 10** interests in a right to die case. The person involved was fully conscious and able to make a decision. The case had attracted a lot of media attention as the woman was a well-known socialite, only aged 50 and not fatally ill. The Daily Mail report referred to the *"socialite who chose death over growing old and ugly"*. The court accepted the woman's decision and allowed treatment to be withdrawn, partly for the reason that she had already made an attempt at suicide. However, it made a restriction order on press coverage to protect the family. This prohibited reporting that could reveal the woman's identity until a further order of the court was made to remove the restriction. The order continued until after her death, including the inquest which is normally public, and the press appealed against it. The court recognised there was a public interest in cases like this, and also in having inquests open and public. However, when balancing this public interest against the private interests of the woman's family, who were already distressed at her death, the scales tipped towards the private interests. A particular factor in the balance was that the youngest daughter had already shown signs of a fragile mental health and the court felt she would suffer further, especially at school, if her mother's identity was revealed. The restriction order was upheld.

In **Campbell**, the HL said there was no difference in the values of **A 8** and **A 10**. In **Middleton 2016**, the HC suggested the circumstances of the case would always be relevant when deciding on the balance. In this case the iCloud account of Pippa Middleton (sister of the Duchess of Cambridge) had been illegally accessed and she sought a court order to prevent any photographs or other data being published prior to bringing a claim in court. In deciding whether or not to make the order the court looked at both sides of the arguments and at the circumstances. The court held that her arguments that her right to a private life under **A 8** would be infringed if the order was not made were *"very strong"*. In contrast, any argument that **A 10** would be infringed if the court order was made were said to be *"very weak"*.

The digital age has increased the availability and accessibility of information. The difficulty this raises is illustrated in **Middleton** above, and again in **PJS v NGN Ltd 2016**. Here the HC granted an injunction to prevent the Sun publishing the name of an entertainer who was having extra-marital sex with another couple. The Sun had said *"The law is an ass"* and complained that his right to cheat beat the rights of the Sun's readers to know about it. The CA allowed the appeal by the Sun and the case went to the SC. The SC ruled that the injunction should remain to give some protection to the children and said that even though the story may be of interest to members of the public, there was no public interest as such in *"kiss and tell"* stories. The difficulty of enforcing injunctions in a digital age should not mean that no injunction should be granted. The information may be *"out there"* but it has to be searched for. It is not as easily accessible as being in the tabloid press and displayed on a newspaper stand. The CA had said that the balance between **A 8** and **A 10** had been correctly applied by the HC but decided that circumstances had changed because in a digital age it is hard to keep matters private and the names had been reported on social media. Therefore the rights now carried different weights when balanced. The man's **A 8** rights had been reduced and the injunction should be lifted. The SC disagreed and held that the public interest element was minimal. His **A 8** rights should therefore prevail and the injunction continue.

Task 29

Pia is the Minister for Children and Families. One day Sven, a reporter, sees her booking into a hotel with another woman's husband. He takes some pictures on his mobile phone and then passes these to the Daily Globe. The newspaper asks him to get some more information and then they will run a story using his pictures. While Sven is investigating he discovers that Pia's daughter has been attending a drug treatment centre and gives the paper the details of her treatment. If Pia wants to stop publication of either of these matters what can she do? Do you think she will succeed?

In **NT v Google** the HC again made clear that neither privacy nor freedom of expression had precedence over the other. The conflict was to be resolved by *"an intense focus on the comparative importance of the specific rights being claimed in the individual case"*.

Examination pointer

You don't need to learn every case, choose a few that make sense to you and consider how the court interpreted the right and whether there was a justified restriction on it, e.g., that it was in the public interest and necessary. Look carefully at the facts, if a child was involved **A 8** will carry more weight (**Weller/Murray**) whereas if there is a genuine public interest, **A 10** will (**Ferdinand**). Where there is both the balance may be more difficult (**Von Hannover**).

Remember that **s 12 HRA** imposes an obligation on courts to *"have particular regard to the importance of the Convention right to freedom of expression"* where the material published is *"journalistic, literary or artistic"*. This would include not only written material but films, painting, radio, television and other such arts as long as they do not contravene the other laws such as those on obscenity, racial hatred etc. Under **s 12** the court should take into account the extent to which the material is already in the public domain and the extent to which it would be in the public interest for the material to be published. The UK courts have not always allowed **A 10** to override **A 8** rights.

Examples

In **Campbell** and **Middleton** the SC made clear that **A 10** should not necessarily carry extra weight and the court must look at all the circumstances.

In **PJS**, the SC held that just because something is already in the public domain and accessible via the internet does not mean publication in the printed press should be allowed. The SC also stated that the public interest element was minimal in such *"kiss and tell"* stories. These may be of interest to the public but this was not the same as being of public interest.

PJS shows that the courts were in disagreement over this issue so is a useful one to use to support an argument either way. The HC favoured suppressing publication, the CA allowed the newspaper's appeal so favoured allowing publication but the SC rejected this and agreed with the HC that publication should be prohibited.

Summary of the way these two rights are balanced

The conflict between these two articles makes for a difficult balancing act.
- In **Campbell v MGN 2004** the HL produced a two-part test which asks to questions to help this balancing act
    - The first question is whether the person claiming violation of **A 8** has an expectation of privacy
    - The second is to balance the two rights
- In **Von Hannover v Germany 2012**, the ECtHR set down five things to take into consideration for this second part.
    - the contribution made by the material to the debate of general interest
    - how well known the person was and the subject of the report
    - the prior conduct of the individual concerned
    - the content, form and consequences of publication
    - the circumstances in which the photo was taken

These will help the court to decide which right will prevail. Here are a few examples from cases already used.

Case	For A 8	For A 10	Which prevailed
A v B 2000	The article was about a private matter, although not a family relationship	It was not a family relationship; he was a well-known footballer	A 10
Murray v Express Newspapers 2008	The pictures were of a child; they were taken without permission	The mother was the author of the famous Harry Potter books	A 8
Ferdinand v MGN Ltd 2011	The article was about a private matter, although not a family relationship	There was a genuine public interest; he was a well-known footballer as captain of England; he had given the impression that he was a family man	A 10
Von Hannover v Germany 2012	The photographs were a private matter and involved her children	There was a genuine public interest; she was a well-known figure	A 10
Weller v Associated Newspapers 2015	It was a family outing and his children were included	There was a genuine public interest; he was a well-known figure	A 8
PJS v NGN Ltd 2016	It was a private relationship; although not a family relationship, there were children involved	He was a well-known figure; the information was already available	A 8
Middleton 2016	The photographs and data were private and had been obtained illegally	She was a well-known figure; there was a genuine public interest	A 8
V v Associated Newspapers and others 2016	It was a private decision; publication could distress her family and affect the health of her child	She was a well-known figure; there was a public interest; inquests should be public	A 8

Task 30

Chose a case from the table above and briefly explain the facts. Then explain what the ECtHR suggested in **Von Hannover** would help decide on the balance and apply these to the facts. Finally, note where the court decided the balance lay.

Although the most obvious conflict between rights is seen between **A 8** and **A 10**, a balance is also needed between **A 10** and **A 11**. This is because a demonstration or protest may also be regarded as a statement.

Case example

In **Sheffield City Council v Fairhall and others 2017**, protesters had prevented a council from felling trees during road improvements. The council sought an injunction to stop them. The protesters argued they had rights under both **A 10** and **A 11**. The HC accepted that the protest was intended to make a powerful statement about the issue of tree removal. This brought it within **A 10**. The protest was clearly an assembly so came within **A 11** as well.

The HC held that the unauthorised entry into the zone where the council was working amounted to trespass. The court added that not every action that constituted a trespass was necessarily outside the scope of **Articles 10** and **11** and much depended on the circumstances. The lawfulness of a protest relying on **Article 10** or **11** rights could change, so that a legitimate protest could, over a period of time, become unlawful. The protest had been disrupting the council's road maintenance work for months and the public interest, as decided by a democratically elected council, should prevail over the rights of the protesters. The court allowed the injunction

Enforcement of human rights

This section should not prove too difficult as there are not many new cases. We will look at how and where rights may be enforced mostly by using cases from previous chapters or from areas of law you have studied elsewhere, such as crime and tort. We will consider the effect of these cases and whether a remedy was provided. There may be one or two which are new to you but these are merely further examples to clarify the way the law works in practice. There are four types of case that may involve claiming a right:

- cases brought in the ECtHR against the state that has violated a right
    - relying on the **ECHR**
    - only after all domestic remedies have been exhausted
- cases brought in the domestic court against a public authority that has violated a right
    - relying on **s 6** and **s 7 HRA**
- cases brought in the domestic court against an individual or organisation in some other kind of action, e.g., an action for false imprisonment or defamation
    - relying on the ordinary national law but the court must take human rights into account under **s 2** and **s 3 HRA**
    - a court is also a public authority so is obliged by **s 6** to act in a way that is compatible with human rights
- cases brought in the domestic court by way of judicial review to test the legality of the power used by a public official
    - relying on the national law, but again the court must take human rights into account

In case you skipped the introduction here is an explanation of the different types of court case.

Civil cases are between the *claimant* (C) and the *defendant* (D), e.g., Smith v Jones 2017.

Judicial review cases are an application to a court to challenge the legality of state decisions or use of powers by public officials which may infringe certain rights. They are in the form *R (on the application of the Smith) v the government department* (or other body against whom the case is brought). The part in brackets *"on the application of Smith"* means that Smith is the person applying for a review of the law. Again these can be abbreviated to surnames.

Human rights cases may be ordinary court cases or by way of judicial review in the national court, as above. However, if the case is taken to the European Court of Human Rights it is in the form *Smith v UK*.

Before going on to the different types of claim here is a general point on English law provisions in regard to human rights. There is a special body set up to monitor and strengthen human rights in the UK, called the Equality and Human Rights Commission. This was established under the **Equality Act 2006**. It operates independently of government and aims to:

- promote awareness, understanding and protection of human rights
- encourage public authorities to comply with the **Human Rights Act**

Claims before the ECtHR

The European Court of Human Rights (ECtHR) is a permanent court set up to guarantee to all citizens of the participating states the rights secured by the **ECHR**. Judges are elected by the Committee of Ministers from across the states but should be independent of their own countries when passing judgment. The court is open to states and individuals regardless of nationality.

Protocol 11 came into force in 1998 and established a single, full-time Court to replace the Commission and ECtHR. It makes the right of individual petition and the jurisdiction of the court compulsory and indefinite for participating States.

The ECtHR will attempt to reach a friendly settlement with the state concerned. If no agreement is reached it will go on to examine the merits of the application. The Committee of Ministers will supervise the execution of the judgment if the claim succeeds.

A 41 of the **ECHR** provides that if a state is in breach but does not allow for a complete remedy the ECtHR can *"afford just satisfaction to the injured party"*. This may include compensation for loss caused by the breach. However, it is up to the state to provide the remedy and this does not always happen. The Committee of Ministers has a supervisory role in enforcing judgments of the court. It will discuss how best to give effect to the judgment with the state and if necessary can issue a resolution or decision requiring a state to comply. This is not always effective. Here is an example where there was no *"just satisfaction"* for the injured party.

Key case

In **Hirst** the ECtHR ruled that **A 8** was breached and that it *"will be for the United Kingdom Government in due course to implement such measures as it considers appropriate to fulfil its obligations to secure the right to vote in compliance with this judgment"* and to provide the applicant *"with just satisfaction."* The UK government ignored the ruling, so the judgment was not of much comfort to Hirst.

The **HRA** did not help as the **Representation of the People Act 1983** could not be interpreted to comply under **s 3**. It clearly provided that a person serving a custodial sentence was *"incapable of voting at any parliamentary or local election"*. That is why the case had to go to the ECtHR having exhausted domestic procedures.

Key points: the ECtHR can order a state to provide just satisfaction but has no real enforcement powers. **S 3 HRA** will not help if the relevant English law is clear.

In **Malone v UK 1984**, the ECtHR ruled that interception of telephone communications breached **A 8** and although the law changed it was made more intrusive. That was before the **HRA** but the situation could still be the same today. It is for the national court to provide a remedy and if the national law is in conflict and that conflict cannot be "interpreted away" the most the court can do is issue a declaration of incompatibility under **s 4**.

The Committee of Ministers can issue a decision requiring a state to comply, but this may be of little practical value. The Committee has issued several decisions since **Hirst** stating that the general, automatic and indiscriminate restriction on the right of convicted prisoners to vote fell outside any acceptable margin of appreciation. It issued such a decision prior to the 2010 UK general election because the ban was still in place, affecting a huge number of people. However, although the UK has recognised it is in breach and that it is required to amend the law, nothing has materialised. Debates and discussions have taken place and promises made, but as for amending the law, that is yet to happen.

Hirst was the focus of **Greens and MT v UK 2010**, although this case was brought under **A 3** of **Protocol 1**, which provides the right to free elections. The ECtHR again ruled that the UK should amend the **1983 Act** and this time ordered the state to pay 5,000 Euros compensation in *"just satisfaction"*.

In a document containing FAQS the ECtHR answers the question *"Are States bound by judgments against them?"* as follows:

"Judgments finding violations are binding on the States concerned and they are obliged to execute them. The Committee of Ministers of the Council of Europe monitors the execution of judgments, particularly to ensure payment of the amounts awarded by the Court to the applicants in compensation for the damage they have sustained".

This is the theory, but **Hirst** shows that it may not be the practice. You can see that whether or not a right is upheld by the ECtHR, much depends on the co-operation of the state as regards whether the claim is satisfied.

Evaluation pointer

Decisions of the ECtHR are not enforceable by the person whose right has been violated. Some claimants may get just satisfaction from a ruling in their favour. However, in other cases compensation may be sought for violation of a right. As there is no effective enforcement mechanism, even if the ECtHR rules that a state is in breach there may be no remedy. The only sanction against the state would be expulsion and that would be politically improbable and of no help to the claimant.

The effect of a successful case in the ECtHR on the state and claimant

The effect for the state is usually a fine. The effect for the claimant may be one of three possibilities:

- the law changes to comply with the right
- compensation is ordered to be paid for violating the right
- nothing happens at all, as in **Hirst**

Claims in the domestic courts

If the right is protected by a national law then a case can be brought using the normal procedures, e.g., for breach of confidence as in **Campbell** or misuse of private information as in the **Google** cases. A writ of *habeas corpus* is still a way of challenging restrictions on the right liberty and the right to a trial, though it is rarely used now. Pre-trial detention is mainly covered by other laws such as **PACE**. In all cases the court must comply with **s 2** and **3 HRA** so will consider human rights when applying the national law.

A claim using national law can be against a public body or an individual. In addition, all the normal remedies will be available, e.g., damages in compensation or an injunction to prevent the violation continuing or a writ of *habeas corpus* to order the person be brought to trial.

Example

If there is a violation of the right to liberty under **A 5** a claim of damages for false imprisonment could be made. *Habeas corpus* would also be appropriate in respect of **A 5 (3)** if the person was not brought promptly before a judge.

If the right is not protected by other national laws **s 7 HRA** can be used to bring a claim in the domestic courts. This is because under **s 6** public authorities must act compatibly with the **ECHR**. **S 6** only applies to public authorities not to individuals. It is an important tool in asserting rights, though. Previously, judicial review proceedings were the only way to challenge decisions of public authorities. Since the **HRA** a victim can rely on a right directly against a public authority under **s 7**. The term public authority includes bodies whose functions are of a public nature. This could include a private company if acting in a public capacity. An example would be a private security service being used to transport prisoners.

In many cases using other domestic law is better. A claim using the **HRA** is limited in that an award of damages, i.e., monetary compensation, is not usually payable. The requirement under **A 41 ECHR** is that the national court provides the claimant with "*just satisfaction*" and **s 8 HRA** provides that the court may only award compensation where it is satisfied that the award is necessary to afford just satisfaction. In **DSD and another 2018** the SC noted that claims under the **ECHR** are different to domestic civil actions. The first are intended to uphold minimum human rights and to vindicate those rights, whereas the latter are designed to compensate claimants for any losses.

When producing the rules of practice for English courts just satisfaction has been interpreted as meaning equitable. The rules make clear that **A 41** does not apply automatically and that the word "*just*" is used in the sense of equitable. This means the circumstances will be important and, as in all English cases, if the claimant has been at fault in any way an equitable remedy may be refused.

The rules of practice also state that a court may decide that the finding of a violation of rights "*is itself sufficient just satisfaction, without there being any call to afford financial compensation.*" This may well be the case where a claim has been made as a matter of principle. However, it will not satisfy many claimants.

Task 31

Andre works for the National Health Service. He is sacked for speaking out against work practices.

Sven works for a private hospital and is sacked for the same reason.

Can either of them bring a claim under the **HRA**?

As the **ECHR** was not part of domestic law until the **HRA** came into force people who wanted to enforce their rights had to take the matter up in Europe by way of a petition to the European Commission of Human Rights (now to the ECtHR). As shown above, this has limited effect if the state is not cooperative.

Since the **HRA** came into force in 2000 many cases are settled in the UK without people having to go to the expense and trouble of taking a case to Strasbourg, as in **Bellinger**.

There are three main ways the **ECHR** may be enforced in the domestic courts.

- **S 2** of the **HRA** requires judges to take account of decisions of the ECtHR
- **S 3** requires judges to interpret national legislation a way which is compatible with the **ECHR** if possible
- **S 6** and **s 7** create a statutory tort whereby individuals affected can claim **ECHR** rights for non-compliance, but only against public authorities

Cases against a public authority may also be by way of judicial review of a decision-making process (see below).

A court is a public authority so must take account of human rights in *all* cases they hear. This is because they have an obligation under **s 6** not to act in a way that is incompatible with human rights. The effect of this is that cases against individuals can involve human rights, not only cases against public authorities. However, in these cases the claim must be based on an existing domestic law not directly on the **HRA**, which merely strengthens that law.

Here is a reminder of the effect of the **HRA** from Chapter 2.

- **S 7** has vertical direct effect (individual against the state)
- It does not have direct horizontal effect (between individuals)
- It may have indirect effect because:
  - there is an existing cause of action in domestic law and the courts must interpret this to comply with the **ECHR** as far as is possible (**s 2 HRA**)
  - public authorities includes courts and tribunals so judges must act in compatibility with the **ECHR** in all cases, whether against a public body or an individual (**s 6**)
  - An example is the development of the tort of misuse of private information from breach of confidence (**Campbell/Google**).

All claims of violation of a right are first attempted by way of the domestic court procedures and remedies. Following the **HRA** this is still a requirement for all cases. The claimant is usually relying on domestic law but supported by the **ECHR** or a ruling of the ECtHR.

Case examples

In **Campbell v MGN 2004** the claim was for breach of confidence but supported by the right to respect for a private and family life under **A 8**. If the HL had not allowed the claim she could then have petitioned the Commission for her case to be heard by the ECtHR as discussed above. That is because the HL was the highest UK court so she had exhausted all domestic possibilities. In fact MGN did petition the ECtHR because the publisher wanted to challenge the decision of the HL and the case had already gone to the highest English court.

The ECtHR decision in **HL v UK 2004** was followed by the national courts in the **Cheshire** case. The SC held that deprivation of liberty must be subject to regular independent checks. This is relying on domestic law based on an earlier decision of the ECtHR. The domestic law had provided for safeguards for anyone deprived of liberty in the **Mental Capacity Act** and these had not been followed. The SC established a test as to what amounted to a deprivation of liberty (and so made a person subject to the **Act**). The SC is the highest national court so this sets a precedent which will be followed by all other domestic courts in the future.

So, a claim before the domestic court is based on English law, either a specific law such as breach of confidence or on **s 7 HRA**. If there is a remedy available, e.g., damages for breach of confidence as in **Campbell**, that is fine. There is no need for the case to go to Strasbourg. Similarly, if the decision is that the English law doesn't quite comply but can be interpreted to do so under **s 3 HRA**, taking into account decisions of the ECtHR as required by **s 2**, then again all is well and there is no need for the case to go to Strasbourg. However, despite the fact that the SC says on its website that *"In giving effect to rights contained in the ECHR the Court must take account of any decision of the ECtHR in Strasbourg"*, there are times when it is not possible to reconcile the laws. If that is the case the UK court will issue a declaration under **s 4** that the law is incompatible.

The effect of a decision in the UK courts on the state and claimant

The effect of decisions in the UK courts for the state is that it may amend the law. As stated earlier, the SC notes on its website that a declaration *"sends a clear message"* that the law should change, so the government may be persuaded to amend it. However, the SC also notes that a declaration imposes no legal obligation to do so.

The effect for claimants depends on what the decision was and whether it was based purely on the national law or on **s 7 HRA**. In the first case the remedy is whatever is normal for breach of that particular law. In the second case the court must provide *"just satisfaction"* under **A 41**.

Examples

In **Campbell** her claim for breach of confidence succeeded and the HL awarded her £3,500. She was awarded damages as compensation for the violation of her right.

In **Miranda**, the CA issued a declaration of incompatibility between stop and detention powers allowed under the **Terrorism Act 2000** and **A 10**. Although he received no remedy the effect was a change in the law to restrict the powers under the **2000 Act**, so this would not happen in the future. This may have provided him with *"just satisfaction"*.

In **Hirst**, the HL issued declaration of incompatibility but this did not lead to a change in the law. The effect for the claimant was zero so he is unlikely to feel he received *"just satisfaction"*

If the national court does not provide a remedy then the claimant will have to appeal up to and including the SC and then petition the ECtHR if no remedy is achieved by the time the national procedure has been exhausted.

Task 32

TP Services is a private security company employed by the government to provide prison guards in Liverpool. The company also provides bodyguards to protect visiting pop stars.

Tom and Terry both work for TP Services. Tom works at the prison and Terry at the homes of pop stars. They have both recently discovered that their boss has been tracking their mobile phone data and want to know if they have any claim against TP Services.

Can either of them bring a claim and if so would it be based on the **HRA** or **A 8 ECHR**?

Claims by way of judicial review

Claims in the domestic courts, whether under ordinary domestic law or under **s 7**, can result in the judge declaring national legislation to be incompatible with rights under the **ECHR**. However, the legislation remains in force until and unless repealed. In some cases judicial review may be the best option. Judicial review can be used to challenge delegated legislation. If this is incompatible with a right and goes beyond the powers of the enabling Act the judge has the power to quash it. Another difference is that only individuals, or victims, can rely on **s 7 HRA** whereas a judicial review case can be brought by anyone with sufficient interest in the issue, which includes pressure groups.

Review proceedings are usually brought in the HC by the Crown (hence the R, as in criminal cases) on an application by the person or group who wishes to challenge the legality of the law or power used. The part of the HC which deals with judicial review is the Administrative Court in the Queen's Bench division. For the sake of brevity I have just used HC. As you know from studying controls on delegated legislation, the judge is being asked to review the decision-making process of a government minister or public authority and rule whether the decision was made within the powers given or was *ultra vires* (beyond the power). The court may decide it was illegal, irrational or irregular. In the first case the decision may be quashed because the power exercised was not authorised by Parliament. The illegal decision will be declared invalid and the minister or public official who made it will have to think again. A judge cannot declare an Act of Parliament invalid; this only applies to secondary legislation and decision-making. In the second case the decision can be quashed if it is so unreasonable no normal public body would have made it. Both of these are substantive *ultra vires* and the court can make an order to quash the decision, or make an order that some action be taken. In the last case the decision can also be quashed but if the official makes the same decision using the correct procedure then it will be valid. This is procedural *ultra vires*.

In a judicial review case the applicant can rely directly on the **HRA** because the case will be against a public authority. The review procedure protects people from the arbitrary use of power by those acting in an official capacity. However, it is a review of the process not the policy itself. The judge cannot say the policy or decision is wrong so should be invalid, only that the person making it either did not have the power to do so or did not follow the correct procedure. The person bringing the case must have *"sufficient interest"* in the matter under review.

Examples (using their short names) already covered include:

- **Moos** on public order law challenging police powers and the use of kettling
- **Laporte** on public order challenging police powers on breach of the peace
- **Purdy** on assisted dying challenging the prosecution guidelines on **s 2 Suicide Act 1961**

Task 33

Using the cases in the list above explain which article was relied on and whether it was breached. Add which court the case would be heard in.

Remember that a court is a public authority so a judicial review of a judge's decision or sentence is possible.

Example

In **Barker v RSPCA 2018**, a couple sought a judicial review of a sentence for breach of the **Animal Welfare Act** which prohibited them from keeping any animal for a period of seven years, with the exception of terrapins. The HC held that the sentence was neither arbitrary nor disproportionate (it allowed for the exception of terrapins) so did not violate **A 8**.

The effect of judicial review decisions on the state and claimant

The effect of decisions in the UK courts for the state is that the policy or decision has to be reviewed. The state will have to amend it to conform to the power given by Parliament or will have to follow the required procedure.

As with a declaration of incompatibility a successful review does not necessarily mean a remedy for the claimant. The court can declare that the power used under the law was *ultra vires* and that a ministerial decision is invalid. This is effective as far as substantive *ultra vires* goes because the court can make an order to quash the decision or an order for the state, or minister of state, to do something to correct it. The law or policy would be invalid and have to be redrawn and the person affected will probably have got *"just satisfaction"*. However, if the court rules that the decision is procedurally wrong all a minister has to do is remake the decision using the correct procedure. In addition, a judge cannot rule that an Act of Parliament is invalid and must be amended.

Example

In **(R (on the application of Purdy) v DPP 2009)**, the court ruled that the DPP must produce an offence-specific policy and this led to an improved set of guidelines. However, there have been many cases since arguing that a lack of clarity remains.

Summary

- If the claim is against a public authority it can be in reliance on **s 7 HRA**
- If the claim is against an individual it can only be in reliance on ordinary domestic law
  - but can be strengthened by use of **s 2** or **s 3 HRA**
- If all else fails a petition can be made to the ECtHR

The main thing to note is that the effect, i.e., the remedy and enforcement of it depends on the type of case.
- In the ECtHR the effect for the state is usually a fine and the effect for the claimant is that the law may be amended or compensation is paid (or nothing happens)
- In the national court the remedy is usually damages or an injunction for the claimant as is normal for breach of the domestic law and the state may amend the law (but is not obliged to)
- If the case is based on the **ECHR** the court must provide *"just satisfaction"* under **A 41**. This may include national remedies but may only be a declaration under **s 4**
- In a judicial review case the court can declare that the power used was *ultra vires* and make an order to quash the decision or an order to do something. The effect may be a change of state policy but may only be remaking the same policy but following the correct procedure

Self-test questions

1. In **Campbell** the HL said there are two matters to consider in cases where **A 8** and **A 10** were in conflict. What are they?
2. In which case did the ECtHR set down five things to take into consideration when balancing **A 8** and **A 10** in respect of the publication of photographs?
3. What English law was **Google v Vidal-Hall** 2015 based on?
4. In which case did the court note that the **Campbell** case had identified the tort of misuse of private information and that the two questions applied to this tort too?
5. In what way does **A 10** overlap with **A 11**?
6. What is horizontal effect and what English provision allows for this?

Chapter 7 criticisms of human rights in the UK and proposals for reform

Overview

Despite the fact that the UK was not only one of the early signatories to the **ECHR** but also helped to draft it, human rights have been the subject of much criticism. In some cases this is based on the argument that the UK adequately protects such rights in its own laws (see Chapter 2). In others it is because rights under the **ECHR** and judgments of the ECtHR are seen as interference by Europe and European judges on UK laws and parliamentary sovereignty. The **HRA** was meant to deal with such arguments by bringing the rights "*home*" and joining them with UK law. This has not been entirely effective in securing rights because even though domestic courts should take account of ECtHR decisions under **s 2** they do not have to follow them. In fact they cannot do so if the domestic law cannot be interpreted to comply under **s 3**.

The **HRA** was introduced by a Labour government and the Conservative government has mostly been against it. The Conservatives have criticised the **HRA** and intimated that ECtHR decisions are binding. Among other criticisms the government has suggested that this has led to it being prevented from deporting terrorists and murderers, and being forced to give prisoners the vote.

When she was Home Secretary, Theresa May said that an illegal immigrant could not be deported because he had a cat. The decision of the court (the UK court by the way) that the man could not be deported was based on the fact that the UK Border Agency had not followed the proper procedure, not the fact that the man had a cat. The cat only got a mention in court as one small part of the evidence of a stable relationship and was not even mentioned in the appeal court. The media don't help; it is easy to see how public misconceptions arise due to coverage of human rights cases in some parts of the press. Apart from the story about the cat (referred to as "Catgate" in some newspapers) there have been a great many other misleading reports. One example is when the Daily Mail reported that a prisoner had the "*human right*" to a KFC Bargain Bucket and cola. In response to questions the police said this was given as part of negotiations with a prisoner protesting on the roof and had nothing to do with any rights. Another example is the report that the killer of head teacher Phillip Lawrence could not be deported because of **A 8 ECHR**. In fact this decision was based on interpretation of EU law and UK regulations, not the **ECHR** or **HRA**. As for giving prisoners the vote, this was given a lot of adverse coverage and was so unpopular across the political spectrum and with the public that the ruling in **Hirst** has been ignored. Anyway, the ECtHR ruling did not mean prisoners should have the right to vote, as was widely reported. It only meant that the individual should be considered. The point was that it was a blanket ban and applied automatically to all prisoners, irrespective of the length of sentence, the nature of the offence or individual circumstances. Arbitrary laws like this, where there is a general prohibition rather than a decision based on the circumstances, will conflict with human rights because they do not consider the individual. Lord Bingham said in **R (Gillan) v Commissioner of Police of the Metropolis 2006** that the exercise of power by public officials should be governed by clear and accessible rules and not used arbitrarily. He also said that the arbitrary use of power went against the rule of law. As the rule of law is a long-established English convention it is somewhat surprising that so many criticisms of human rights are based on cases where it was the rule of law that lay behind the decision. This chapter will explore some of those criticisms, both of human rights under the **ECHR** and of the **HRA**.

Criticisms of the ECHR and ECtHR

Two of the more vocal criticisms of human right are based on the effect of the **ECHR** and ECtHR decisions on parliamentary sovereignty and domestic policies. In fact, in both cases the effect is very limited. Although early in the EU referendum campaign in 2016 Theresa May said that the **ECHR** binds the hands of the UK Parliament this is only true up to a point. Under **s 19** of the **HRA** every bill put before Parliament must contain a statement saying that it is compatible with the **ECHR** or *that it is not and this was intended*. This means that Parliament will usually make sure that new laws are compatible with **ECHR** rights, but it does not have to.

Suggesting that decisions of the ECtHR are binding and/or affect parliamentary sovereignty misleads the public into thinking that somehow judges in Europe are telling the UK government and the UK people what to do. This is disingenuous because judgments from the ECtHR are not binding and **s 2 HRA** only requires judges to *"take account of"* ECtHR decisions. In addition, **s 3** requires judges to interpret legislation to comply with the **ECHR** but only *"so far as it is possible to do so"*. Decisions of the ECtHR are supposed to be binding on the state (even though not on the courts) but even then it can be seen from **Hirst** that this is not always so in practice. In fact a significant criticism of the current situation from supporters of human rights is that there is no effective enforcement of a right following a decision by the ECtHR. If the applicant is successful any remedy is dependent on co-operation by the state.

So, parliamentary sovereignty is not really affected by either the **ECHR** or the **HRA**. Neither judges in the ECtHR nor the domestic courts can overrule Parliament. Judges in national courts can declare an Act of Parliament to be incompatible with the **ECHR** but that is as far as they can go. They cannot change the law. **Hirst** is an example of this, as are many of the other cases we have looked at. In **Miranda** the UK court issued a declaration of incompatibility with **A 10** because there were inadequate safeguards against the arbitrary exercise of the power. The non-arbitrary use of power and proper independent and impartial scrutiny are part of the rule of law and policies which go against this are likely to fall foul of the **ECHR**.

All citizens of participating states are entitled to the protection of the **ECHR**. However, it is minority groups and vulnerable people who are most in danger of having their rights violated and who are least able to fight this. They are also most likely to be the focus of negative public opinion. Some parts of the media have referred to **A 8** as a *"criminals' charter"*. Prisoners, immigrants and mental patients have few powers to challenge authority and are in a weak position. This is why bodies like Amnesty International and the Howard League for Penal Reform are important, they are there to help those who cannot fight for themselves. Prisoners are in a weak position because they are seen as unworthy of the law's protection. There is some sympathy with this view because they have broken the law. However, another argument which arose in **Hirst** was that the punishment for the crime had already been given in the form of a custodial sentence. There was no argument about whether the right to liberty had been violated. It was accepted that this was properly forfeited by the commission of the crime. The argument was that this did not mean other rights should also be forfeit.

On a more positive note, the SC has said there is a dialogue between it and the ECtHR and this is a promising sign of greater co-operation. This is highlighted by the fact that the ECtHR has followed the SC and not just the other way around, as in in **Al-Khawaja 2011**.

Domestic policies may be affected by human rights but again this is limited. Policies are quite often amended following a case where either the ECtHR or the domestic court has said that it is incompatible with the **ECHR**. However, this happened before the **HRA** as we saw in Chapter

2, e.g., **Golder v UK 1973**. Anyway, amending the policy to conform is not always the case and it is certainly not compulsory, as seen in **Hirst**.

We saw in the overview that much of the criticism is unfounded. However, there are also genuine concerns and any evaluation of human rights law should attempt to consider both sides of the argument.

One argument that has merit is that ECtHR decisions are made by judges and not agreed upon by the participating states. This is a stronger argument than the one about the **ECHR** itself as judge-made law is less democratic than laws made by an elected Parliament. This lack of democracy means that the fact that the ECtHR sees the **ECHR** as a living instrument has both advantages and disadvantages. The advantage is that it allows the law to develop along with advances in technology and changing social attitudes (as seen in the cases on surveillance and transsexuals). On the other hand, as is the case with development of the English common law through precedent, it is undemocratic. In the **Gard** case there was a public outcry following the ruling against the UK because the case had stirred up public opinion which condemned interference from European judges with the child's treatment. However, the UK courts had already decided that doctors should be allowed to withdraw treatment. It was the parents who challenged this in the ECtHR, which agreed with the domestic courts. A more sustainable criticism about decisions of the ECtHR is that there is conflicting case law, a point noted by the SC in **Kennedy**. A related argument is that the fact that judges in domestic courts do not have to follow the ECtHR is a double-edged sword. It may satisfy those who do not want interference from Europe but it also causes conflicting case law, this time between the ECtHR and the national courts. Examples include whether preventative measures are justifiable under **A 5**, and under which subsection and at what stage consideration of the circumstances should take place – to engage a right or to justify it? In **Austin 2009**, the HL did not agree with the ECtHR decision in **Ostendorf** on preventative measures under **A 5** and in **Hicks** the HL did not agree with the ECtHR decision in **Austin 2012** on the stage for consideration of the circumstances.

Examination pointer

These criticisms show there may be two sides to the same point of debate. This is fine as such examples help you to produce a balanced argument. You can illustrate the point with a case or two to show how it has worked in practice. You could, e.g., use **Goodwin** to show how the law needs to keep up with social attitudes and mention that in **Bellinger** the domestic court came to the same decision. Another point you could mention is that public opinion may not always be against ECtHR decisions. It was in **Gard**, but in the **Observer and Guardian v UK 1991** case the public denigrated English judges and called the law an ass. The ECtHR decision was widely applauded.

You could conclude that despite the undemocratic nature of the decisions there is no obligation on the state to follow them. Use **Hirst** in support of the fact that the state can ignore an ECtHR decision altogether and, e.g., **Miranda** to show that even the domestic courts can only make a declaration and not amend the law.

The decision in **Bellinger** was somewhat contentious at the time because opinion was divided. The HL decided that English law did not comply with the **ECHR** but held that it could not interpret English law to make it do so. The ECtHR ruled the law breached **A 8** in **Goodwin** just before the HL decision in **Bellinger** and the law was changed by the **Gender Recognition Act**.

Here the ECtHR and the HL (now the SC) both came to the same conclusion independently. This is arguably a positive thing as it shows the courts are in harmony.

Another contentious area which has seen many cases in both domestic courts and the ECtHR is assisted dying. These cases include criticisms of human rights because although challenging domestic law they are based on rights under the **ECHR**.

Examination of the cases shows that judges are divided on the issue but that most feel it should be a matter for Parliament to change the law. In **R (on the application of Nicklinson and another) v Ministry of Justice 2014**, the SC held unanimously that the question whether the current law on assisted suicide under **S 2 Suicide Act 1961** is incompatible with **A 8** lies within the UK's margin of appreciation, and is therefore a question for the UK courts to decide. However, the court was divided on the question of whether to make a declaration of incompatibility. The argument for doing so was that the court then does what Parliament, through the **HRA**, has empowered them to do, which is to remit the issue to Parliament for a political decision informed by the court's view of the law. The arguments against were not dissimilar, that it was for a democratically elected Parliament to decide. The majority saw the justification for an absolute prohibition on assisted suicide and decided the law was "*necessary*". They noted that there was a risk to the lives of vulnerable individuals who might feel themselves a burden to their family, friends or society and might, if assisted suicide were permitted, be persuaded to undertake it when they would not otherwise do so. The SC declined to make a declaration. It was also noted that an **Assisted Dying Bill** was being debated by Parliament and this influenced the decision. In **Conway 2017**, the facts were narrower as the man had fewer than six months to live. This time the CA recognised the law could be incompatible with his **A 8** rights and allowed a judicial review. However, the HC decided the **Suicide Act** did not violate **A 8** because the law was necessary and justified to protect the weak and vulnerable.

One argument against the **ECHR** made by people on all sides of the debate is that there are too many exceptions. With so many restrictions on the rights it is said that they lack real value. A related argument is that the margin of appreciation given to states by the **ECHR** allows too much discretion and makes the law uncertain.

Another significant criticism of the law as it stands is that it badly needs updating and is out of touch with twenty-first century views. The **ECHR** was drafted a long time ago and in response to the specific circumstances of the post-war years. The **HRA** only brings the rights agreed at the time into domestic law (and, as seen above, not very effectively) and the UK has signed up to very few of the protocols which have gone some way to updating it. There are sound arguments for modernising the law and extending its protection to the environment and to cover children's rights. It would arguably be easier to repeal and replace the **HRA** than to amend it. This is discussed below with reforms but first we will consider the criticisms that have led to the calls for reform.

Criticisms of the HRA

There is a sound argument that the **HRA** should provide for enforceable rights rather than merely imposing an obligation to take account of them. If the rights were directly incorporated into English law they would truly have been brought home. This would help to counter the arguments about interference from Europe.

There are plenty of criticisms which have been made about the **HRA** based on this argument, as well as others which are also valid. They include:

- The **HRA** does not incorporate **ECHR** rights
    - trying to establish violation of a right is time-consuming and costly because attempts at domestic remedies must be exhausted first
    - many human rights are covered by UK laws but these are scattered and hard to ascertain, e.g., much legislation is complex and many rights rely on the common law alone
    - there is no proper enforcement of a right
    - the **HRA** does not provide for human rights it merely provides that politicians and judges must take them into account
- The **HRA** applies to public authorities but this does not include Parliament
    - although it does mean a person can rely on the right directly even though not incorporated into domestic law
- The **HRA** does not apply to private bodies, which leads to inconsistency
    - e.g., people affected by the actions of a National Health Service hospital could claim their rights where if the same thing happened in a private hospital there could be no such claim

Task 34

Evaluation of the law requires you to look at all sides of the debate and not just state one view. The column on the left contains a few arguments for or against the current position on human rights law. Add a brief opposing view to the right-hand column.

Viewpoint	Opposing view
The ECHR usurps parliamentary sovereignty	
Claiming a right is time-consuming because domestic remedies must be tried first	
UK laws are scattered and it is hard to know if the domestic law covers the situation	
The **HRA** does not apply to private bodies	
The margin of appreciation given to states reduces the rights	
There are too many restrictions on many of the rights so they lack real value	

Proposals for reform

We have seen that there are several criticisms of the **HRA** and people from across the political spectrum can see reasons for repealing it. However, repeal of the **HRA** would not affect the UK's international obligation to abide by the **ECHR** (as was the case before the **HRA** became law). That means repeal of the **HRA** would make human rights law more European, not less.

Repeal would cause constitutional difficulties too and it is hard to see how it could succeed because the devolved powers are against it (see Chapter 2). There is concern that any attempt by the Westminster Parliament at reducing rights which affect the devolved powers would lead to constitutional problems and could disturb the Union between the countries involved.

The United Kingdom could cease to be united. It seems that repeal just won't work unless the **HRA** is replaced with something else.

Most proposals for reform focus on repeal of the **HRA** and the introduction of a Bill of Rights. The idea of a Bill of Rights is not new but has received more attention in recent years.

A Bill of Rights – the past and the future

The **Bill of Rights 1689** limited the power of the monarch and put certain freedoms into statutory form but did not go very far. Having a Bill of Rights which ensured proper rights rather than residual freedoms has been discussed at times over the centuries and there have been one or two serious attempts at producing such a document. As stated above, there are valid arguments that the law is out of date and needs to be brought into line with the different needs of the 21st century. This century has seen a new impetus on the subject.

Writing in the Guardian in 2011, the human rights lawyer, Geoffrey Robertson, argued in favour of a British Bill of Rights. He said the case for such a bill had become overwhelming not just as an improvement on the **ECHR** *"but as a powerful symbol of British identity. A reminder to our children, to our immigrants and ourselves, of the struggles in this country to achieve democracy, parliamentary sovereignty, judicial independence, Press freedom, habeas corpus, trial by jury and so forth"*. This type of approach would probably go some way to calming fears of a rights-based culture which follows European ideas. It puts the emphasis firmly on British traditions and rights.

The idea behind a new Bill of Rights is to provide for rights but qualify those rights by reference to domestic interests and values. This would make the residual freedoms enjoyed by UK citizens into positive rights but at the same time might satisfy those who think the **ECHR** goes too far by allowing a wider margin of appreciation to states. An independent parliamentary commission was set up in 2011 to consider a Bill of Rights. Although there was evidence that several commissioners thought that any such document should maintain the **ECHR** rights and even add to them, there was no consensus of opinion.

In 2014, the Conservative government put forward proposals for replacing the **HRA** with a British Bill of Rights. This would be based on the **ECHR** but would be *"limited to cases that involve criminal law and the liberty of an individual, the right to property and similar serious matters"*. It would exclude *"trivial cases"*. This has caused concern because it is by no means clear what would be deemed trivial. It is often rights that appear trivial that most need protecting. As I said earlier, it is minority groups who are most often in danger of violation of their rights, so they need the protection of a robust human rights law. In The Rule of Law (see Chapter 1) Lord Bingham said that the rule of law required legal protection of such human rights as are seen within society as fundamental. He also asks which rights would be discarded by those who are against the **ECHR** and/or the **HRA**. He suggests that although there could be arguments in favour of adding more rights to the **ECHR** none *"could be safely discarded"*.

Proposals for a Bill of Rights were again mentioned in the Queen's speech in 2015 and 2016. Then later in 2016 the government suggested withdrawing from the **ECHR** but remaining in the European Union. Withdrawing from the **ECHR** may not be that popular as it would mean a return to the position pre-1950. Following the leave vote in 2016 the government went into reverse and suggested leaving the EU but sticking with the **ECHR**. Repeal of the **HRA** remained firmly on the agenda though, and the idea of having a British Bill of Rights was still a possibility.

However, things have cooled off since then.

A House of Lords EU Committee reported in 2016 on the proposals for a British Bill of Rights. This noted that the devolved powers were unlikely to give consent to repeal of the **HRA**. Theoretically the UK government could go ahead without consent because when power to legislate was given to the devolved states, overall sovereignty was retained by Westminster. The Sewel convention (see Chapter 2) provides that the UK Parliament will not normally legislate on devolved matters, or matters which could affect the powers of the devolved parliaments, without consent. Going ahead with repeal of the **HRA** is likely to cause constitutional problems if consent is not obtained. This could possibly be avoided if the proposals include replacing it with a Bill of rights which is stronger and enforceable. The problem is getting agreement on what it should contain.

A Bill of Rights passed by Parliament (with the agreement of the devolved powers) would be more acceptable to those concerned that European judges are usurping parliamentary sovereignty. Unlike the **HRA** which does not make any of the rights directly enforceable, a Bill of Rights would more clearly do what the Labour government intended when introducing the **HRA 1998** and *"bring rights home"*.

Here are a few arguments both for and against a Bill of Rights to replace the **HRA**

Arguments for a Bill of Rights

- It would give a clear statement of available rights
- Rights would be just that, rights rather than residual freedoms
- People could rely directly on the Bill of Rights and would not need to go through the current lengthy procedures
- It would give people more power against possible abuses by public authorities, including ministers and members of Parliament
- Most democratic countries have some kind of constitution safeguarding fundamental rights and a Bill of Rights would bring the UK into line
- A Bill of Rights would be a clear sign to those in power that they should act to protect rights and not use power arbitrarily
- It would also be a sign to those in vulnerable positions that they are under the law's protection
- It would send a message to both those wielding power and those affected by it that the UK has a moral code
- It would support parliamentary sovereignty
- It could reduce judicial activism as judges would not need to develop the common law to protect rights
- It could qualify rights more clearly to suit domestic interests
- It could be clearer on how rights should be balanced when in conflict (as **s 12 HRA** does with **A 10**)

Arguments against a Bill of Rights

- UK law adequately protects human rights in various statutes and under common law
- The current system of residual freedoms are not so absolute as claim rights so the law is more flexible
- A Bill of Rights would need to be interpreted by judges who may not be equipped for the task
- The **HRA** was passed by a UK Act of Parliament so supports parliamentary sovereignty

- The **HRA** may not be enforceable but it encourages politicians and judges to consider human rights and allows for flexibility
- A Bill of Rights would be less flexible than the current arrangement by which judges are able to interpret the law to comply with the right quite liberally
- The **ECHR** allows the state a margin of appreciation which makes it more acceptable to the public (but not those affected)
- Under the doctrine of parliamentary sovereignty one Parliament cannot bind a later one which means any Bill of Rights would lack constitutional force
- Rights may be qualified to the extent that they offer little protection
- The only alternative would be to have an entrenched Bill of Rights as in Germany and the USA where it is a higher law. However, that would go against the doctrine of parliamentary sovereignty
- Whether granted under the **ECHR**, the **HRA** or a Bill of Rights, there is no guarantee that the rights would be enforceable against abuse of power (unless entrenched and overriding other laws – but see above)

Conclusion

The early part of this book looked at the history of human rights and showed that the UK led the way in matters such as liberty, the right to life and other freedoms. It introduced *habeas corpus* centuries ago and abolished capital punishment many years before the **ECHR** did. In the first chapter we covered the rule of law, another long-standing English convention. In Lord Bingham's view, the rule of law should protect human rights and comply with international obligations if it is to apply to a modern state. Repeal of the **HRA** would not affect the UK's international obligation to abide by the **ECHR**, as was the case between 1950 and 2000. Repeal without replacement would therefore be a backward step.

On the other hand, if replaced with a tougher piece of legislation, repeal of the **HRA** may lead to increased rather than fewer rights. A Bill of Rights could improve matters because it could be enforceable and up to date. If it strengthens and extends the rights to encompass the young, the elderly and the planet it could be superior to the **ECHR**. Squeals of protest about prisoners being allowed to vote and cats preventing the deportation of illegal immigrants do not serve the public. The discussions and debates would be better to focus on the traditional rights that British citizens have enjoyed and how these might be extended to others in a vulnerable position. The press could help by reporting more accurately and with a little more objectivity.

Perhaps the time is now right for a new Bill of Rights to put human rights into statutory form and make the law fit for the 21st century.

Task 35 and summary

Here is a summary of some arguments from cases we have looked at. See if you can add an opposing argument. This will help you to produce a balanced evaluation.

Viewpoint	Opposing viewpoint
Development of privacy laws go against the freedom of the press (**Campbell** etc.)	
Anti-terrorism laws are needed to protect the nation (The **Belmarsh** case)	
Data protection is needed to protect the individual (**Watson/Andrew**)	
Prisoners should not be allowed to vote (**Hirst**)	
People should be able to put the past behind them (**NT 1 and NT2 v Google**)	

There are no self-test questions as this chapter is mainly a matter of opinion

Chapter 8 Revision and examination practice

Here is a short recap of the main topics followed by examination guidance. This guidance covers specific help for application and evaluation of human rights law plus a general guide to the requirements for the A-level examination.

Revision

When applying the law you need to explain the rights and any exceptions and then consider which English law covers the situation. Most articles impose both a positive duty and a negative duty on the state. **A 5** and **A 6** are limited rights so allow for few exceptions, however **A 8**, **A 10** and **A 11** are qualified rights and paragraph two of each article allows state interference where necessary in a democratic society. You will need to look at whether the state has passed laws to meet its obligations under the **ECHR** and whether any measures taken under these laws amount to a violation of the right or are justified.

A 5 imposes a positive duty to protect liberty (e.g., by laws on false imprisonment) and a negative duty not to deprive someone of liberty (e.g., by ensuring any detention is lawful). This is a limited right and there are exceptions under **A 5 (1)**.

A 6 imposes a positive duty on the state to protect the right to a fair hearing e.g., by laws that grant the right to a solicitor and other procedural rights under **PACE**. The negative obligation is not to interfere with the right and this could be violated by not providing for youth trials (as in **Thompson and Venables**) or not allowing the accused to cross-examine a witness (as in **Davis**).

As with **A 5**, **A 6** is limited right as there are specific exceptions stated in the **ECHR**. **A 6** provides that a trial should be fair, public and independent but allows for the press and public to be excluded in certain circumstances. These include the protection of morals, public order, juveniles, private lives and the interests of justice.

In both cases, the questions to ask when applying the law to **A 5** and **A 6** are:

- Does the measure interfere with a right under the **ECHR**?
    - If so does one of the exceptions apply?
- Under what English law is the measure allowed?

A claim may be under the specific English law or under **s 7 HRA** relying directly on the **ECHR** right. In either case the next questions are:

- Is the measure necessary in a democratic society?
    - Is there a legitimate aim?
    - Is the measure proportionate to the aim?

If so the interference may be justified.

If not the interference may violate the right.

A 8 imposes a positive duty to protect respect for a private life (e.g., by having laws on equalising rights between heterosexuals and gays) and a negative duty not to interfere with someone's private life (e.g., by not having laws allowing for intercepting communications).

A 10 imposes a positive duty to protect freedom of expression (e.g., by laws on freedom of information and **s 12 HRA**) and a negative duty not to interfere with freedom of expression (e.g., by rules allowing for political dissent, scientific debate and other ways to express opinions).

A 11 imposes a positive duty to protect freedom of assembly and association (e.g., by laws restricting police powers to break up such meetings) and a negative duty not to interfere with this freedom (e.g., by not having laws allowing for excessive police interference).

These three rights are qualified. The questions to ask when applying the law are:

- Under what English law is the measure allowed?
- Does the law / measure respect the right to respect for a private life / freedom of expression / freedom of assembly?
  - If not the measure may be an interference with the right

If the English law does not apply there may be a claim under **s 7 HRA** relying directly on the **ECHR** right as long as the claim is against a public authority.

In either case the next questions are:

- Is the measure necessary in a democratic society?
  - Is there a legitimate aim?
  - Is the measure proportionate to the aim?
- If so the interference may be justified
- If not the interference may violate the right

For these three qualified rights the aims stated in paragraph 2 will be legitimate.

Remember too that In **Steinfeld and Keidan 2018** the SC restated the test for justification of a qualified right. As well as asking whether the measure is proportionate to a legitimate aim it asks whether the measure strikes a fair balance between the rights of the individual and the interests of the community.

In all cases, when deciding if the measure complies the court will also consider **s 2** and **s 3 HRA**.

Task 36

Choose a case and apply the law to it in the way set out above, including what effect **s 2, s 3 and s 4 HRA** may have.

Task 37

Match the section of the **HRA** to what it provides

S 2	a court may make a declaration of incompatibility with a Convention right
S 3	every bill put before Parliament must contain a statement saying that it is compatible with the **ECHR** or that it is not and this was intended
S 4	requires judges to read and give effect to national law in a way which is compatible with the **ECHR**
S 6	a court may only award compensation where it is satisfied that the award is necessary to afford just satisfaction
S 7	makes it unlawful for public authorities to act in a way that is incompatible with the **ECHR**
S 8	requires judges to take account of decisions of the ECtHR
S 19	a victim can bring a claim in the domestic courts against a public authority

The **HRA** protects **ECHR** rights by allowing an action under **s 7** against a public authority for non-compatibility. A public authority may breach human rights in two ways:
- By doing something which interferes with the right, e.g., excessive surveillance
- By failing to do something that puts the right at risk, e.g., not protecting the right to speak freely

S 7 provides for vertical direct effect (individual against the state). Only a victim can bring a claim under **s 7** and damages are not usually awarded (**s 8**). There is no horizontal direct effect but protection can be achieved indirectly by interpretation of domestic law to comply (**s 3**) and by taking account of ECtHR decisions (**s2**).

This means enforcement can be through:
- the domestic court against a public authority in reliance on **s 7**
- the domestic court against an individual in reliance on national law but supported by **s 2** and **s 3**
- the domestic court against a public authority by way of judicial review of a decision-making process relying on either **s 7** or domestic law
- the ECtHR against the state but only once all else has failed

Here is the summary diagram from Chapter 2 with a bit added.

Bringing a claim for breach of a right

What it the claim?	What is the law?	The role of the ECtHR?
A claim based on domestic law in a domestic court	Use the relevant domestic law e.g., contempt of court. Support the claim by way of **s 2** and **s 3 HRA**. The claim can be against a public authority or individual. Judicial review of the measure is an alternative against a public authority	If the claim and any appeals fail petition the ECtHR. If the claim is admissible the court will rule as to whether the state has met its obligations under the **ECHR**. If not the claim will succeed and the Commission will order the state to provide just satisfaction
A claim based on the **ECHR** in a domestic court	Use **s 7 HRA**. Support the claim by way of **s 2** and **s 3 HRA**. The claim can only be against a public authority. Judicial review is an alternative	
A claim based on the **ECHR** in the ECtHR	Use the **ECHR** but only if domestic laws have been exhausted	

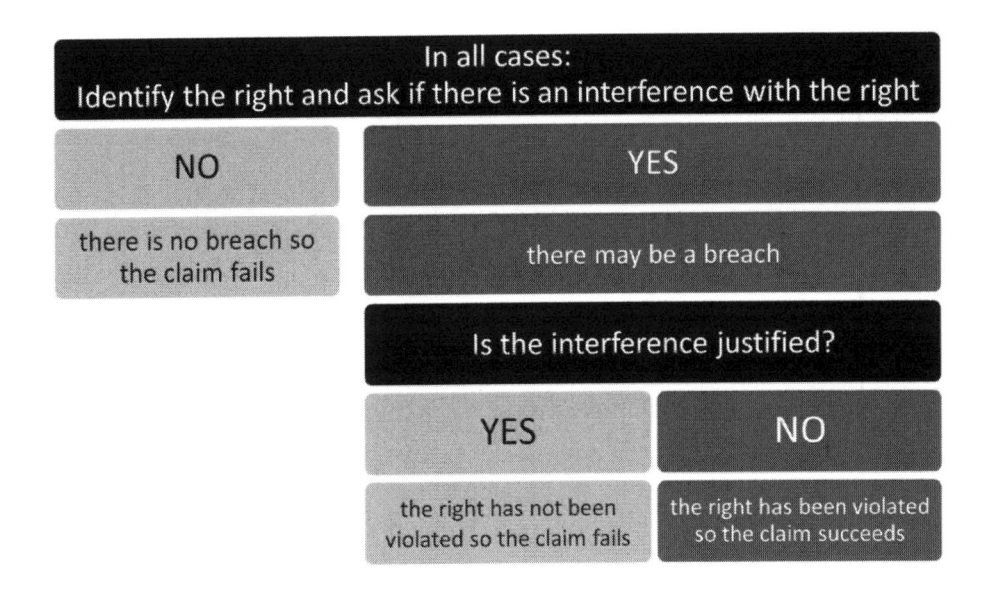

In all cases:
Identify the right and ask if there is an interference with the right

NO — there is no breach so the claim fails

YES — there may be a breach

Is the interference justified?

YES — the right has not been violated so the claim fails

NO — the right has been violated so the claim succeeds

Remember that to be justified the measure that interferes with the right must have a legitimate aim and be proportionate to that aim.

The following table shows the overlap between articles when applying English law (which is why A 2 is included). The middle column gives the most affected articles, there may be others. The case examples are just that, examples. There are plenty of others you could use. In particular, A 8 is so wide that there are few laws that have no effect on this right in some way and there are a huge number of cases.

English law(s)	Article(s)	Case example(s)
Murder, manslaughter, euthanasia and withdrawal of treatment	A 2, A 6 and A 8	Pretty 2002 Foye 2013 Conway 2018
Negligence, protective policing, the use of force and investigations into deaths	A 2 and A 6	Robinson 2018 Murray v UK 1996
Police powers under PACE, SOCPA and CJPOA	A 5, A 6, A 8, A 10 and A 11	Roberts 2015 Miranda 2016 Ibrahim v. the UK 2016
Police powers under the Public Order Act 1986	A 5, A 6, A 10 and A 11	Laporte 2006
Breach of the peace and obstruction of the highway	A 5, A 10 and A 11	Austin 2012 Moos 2012 Hicks 2017 DPP v Jones and Lloyd 1999
Data collection and retention, surveillance and freedom of information	A 8 and A 10	Watson 2018 Gaughran 2015 Kennedy 2014
Breach of confidence and misuse of private information	A 8 and A 10	Campbell 2004 NT1 and NT2 v Google 2018
Defamation and harassment	A 8, A 10 and A 11	Joseph v Spiller 2010 Trimingham v Associated Newspapers 2012
Obscenity, racial hatred, censorship and blasphemy	A 10 and A 11	Gillberg v Sweden 2012 Viscount St Davids 2017

A final point is that although many of the cases on human rights are claims to the right, the **ECHR** and **HRA** can also be used in defence against a civil claim or a prosecution.

Task 38

Now that you have covered the rights briefly explain what the alternatives are and make a note of a case example for each type of claim. Explain the effect of the **HRA** on your chosen examples where appropriate.

Examination guidance

These two examination boards have similar requirements. For Eduqas there are three "Components". Components 2 and 3 are on the substantive law (crime, tort, contract and human rights) and you have to cover three of these four topics. (Component 1 is on the nature of law and the legal system). For human rights (and two other topics) you have to answer an application question in Component 2 and an essay question in Component 3

For OCR the nature of law and substantive law are in the same paper. There are three papers, one for criminal law, one for tort and one for human rights or contract. Each will include two questions on the nature of law and a scenario on the substantive law. Human rights law is on Paper 3 'Further Law'. There will be two questions in Section A of the paper on the nature of law and you must answer one. In Section B there will be two scenarios on human rights and you need to choose one of these and answer all three questions on it. Two application questions and one essay.

For both boards each question is worth 25 marks.

What you need for application and essay questions cannot be divided completely but there is a difference. For both, it is important to know and understand cases and principles well. This is because the examination is not merely a test of knowledge; it is a test of your ability to *use* that knowledge, whether in applying what you know to a set of facts, or in evaluating what you know and offering a critique of the law.

In either case, you should structure your answer. As this is a test of **law** you need to state the legal principles involved and apply them to the particular question. A solid start is worth a lot and gets the examiner on your side.

Don't be tempted to write all you know about the area. Being selective is a skill in itself and an examiner won't be able to give you marks for stuff that isn't relevant, even if it is correct. If you ask a solicitor for advice, they won't tell you everything they know, they will pick out the law that suits your case. You have to do the same in answering an examination question.

In precedent, you learnt that the important part of a case is the *ratio decidendi*, the reasoning behind the judge's decision. As you revise a case, think about this and look for the legal principle.

It is important to:

Explain a case briefly but show that you understand the principle

Show that you understand the law well enough to be selective by only referring to the relevant facts

Application advice

For application of the law to a scenario (problem questions) you need to take a logical approach. Read the scenario carefully to make sure you understand what it is about. Sometimes you will be directed to a specific right and sometimes not. It may be necessary to discuss more than one as there is often an overlap. However, if you are told to discuss a particular right you cannot get marks for discussing any others. Read the questions carefully to see if you are being directed to a particular right. If not discuss all possibilities.

Try to summarise the facts in a few words. This is valuable when time is short. The principle of the case is the important part, although you may need to discuss the facts briefly to show why you have chosen that particular case.

Example

Here are the facts again of a case involving **A 6**.

In **Murray v UK 1996** the ECtHR ruled that **s 34** did not violate **A 6**. Unlike the situation in America, where the right to silence is a fundamental right under the US Constitution, no such right exists in the UK, where the law is based on residual freedoms rather than rights. However, in the same case, the ECtHR ruled that denying a prisoner access to a solicitor for 48 hours was in breach of **A 6**. In deciding whether **A 6** is breached in such situations, much will depend on the facts. The length of time will be one such factor.

The principle is that denial of access to a solicitor may breach **A 6**. If the examination scenario involves denial of access to a solicitor for a certain amount of time you would pick up on this fact. You might say *"In **Murray v UK 1996** the ECtHR ruled that denying a prisoner access to a solicitor for 48 hours was in breach of **A 6**"* and then go on to discuss the length of time and whether it was proportionate in the circumstances.

If you can't remember the name of a case that is relevant don't leave it out but refer to it in a general way, e.g., 'in one decided case...' or 'in a similar case...'

You need to use *current* and *relevant* legal rules, which come from statutes or cases. Use the **examination pointers** plus the **diagrams** or **summaries** at the end of each chapter as a guide to the important points to know. An answer should be rounded off with a conclusion where possible. You should never start an answer with *"there is a violation of Article X"*. What you need to do is to use the law to prove it.

With human rights you need to take the same logical approach as for any other subject but don't forget you are likely to have to discuss both human rights law and domestic law.

Firstly, identify which right is involved. Secondly, consider whether the right has been engaged. Thirdly, discuss which domestic law is involved. Then discuss the exceptions and whether any restrictions are:

- prescribed by or in accordance with law
- for a permitted purpose
- necessary in a democratic society
- proportionate to the purpose (or aim)

Look at the answer to Task 36 as a guide and ensure you cover the following points.

Identify the appropriate area of law – this will tell the examiner you have understood the focus of the scenario and will shape your answer.

Apply the relevant rules in a logical way to the facts – this will be the substance of your answer. Define the right and restrictions on it then take each of these in turn. Do this for each right if there is more than one. If you do this logically you won't leave anything out.

Which law? – discuss which national law covers the situation if there is one. If not discuss a possible action under **s 7 HRA** if a public authority is involved.

Add a little more detail if there is a particular issue shown by the facts – there will often be something particular to focus on so look for clues in the given facts to see if you need more on anything, e.g., justification and/or proportionality.

Support your application with relevant cases – only use cases which are relevant to the particular scenario, and only state those facts that are essential to show the examiner why you have chosen that case, e.g., because the facts are similar.

Conclude in a way that is sustainable and supported by what you have said and the cases you used – it is useful to look back at the question at this point. If it says, "*Advise Mary ...*", you should make sure that your answer does so. In your conclusion, you should pull together the different strands of your answer and then say that based on that application "*I would advise Mary that ...*".

Examination pointer

I repeat the following pointer from Chapter 3 as it can be adapted to apply to other rights too. It is useful if you are unsure whether to consider the circumstances in order to see if the right is engaged (**Austin**) or in order to see if the right was breached (**Hicks**).

The fact that the law is not clear as regards at what stage you need to consider the circumstances means you can point to **Austin** and **Hicks** and say "*there may not be any interference with the right because it was short term and the purpose was to prevent violence (Austin), but if there is then the circumstances need to be looked at (Hicks) ...*" and go on to discuss whether there is a breach or whether the interference is justified.

Finally, it is good policy to refer to the facts of a scenario as often as you can when applying the law as this indicates that you are answering the specific question and have a sound enough knowledge of law and legal principles to know which cases are relevant to the particular facts. It also helps to keep you focused. Examiners usually include pointers either to which right is engaged or whether the situation raises a particular issue. Always look for clues and take each issue in turn.

Task 39 application practice

Piotr works behind the bar in a strip club. He notices that a customer sitting close to the pole dancing area is Max Markham, a local MP who campaigns vociferously against pornography. Piotr uses his mobile phone to take secret pictures of Max as he tucks some money into the pole-dancer's garter at the end of her act. He plans to sell these to the town's weekly newspaper. Advise Max whether he can use **s 7 HRA** to secure an injunction to prevent publication and what alternatives he may have.

Evaluation advice

Essays require more discussion and evaluation of the law or legal issues. The criticisms in the previous chapter will help with this, along with the ***evaluation pointers***.

In an essay question, you may need to form an opinion or weigh up arguments about a particular area of law, or a certain principle or issue. Here a broader range of knowledge is needed, showing you understand any problems with the law and are able to assess these and discuss possible reforms. You should always round off your answer with a short concluding paragraph, preferably referring back to the question. This shows the examiner you are addressing the given question and not one you would have preferred to have been asked. Planning an evaluation answer on an area of law is fine, as long as you are prepared to adapt it to the specific question. Not doing so is a common failing on which examiners' reports frequently comment.

Example

If the examination question asks you to discuss both criticisms and reforms, make sure both these words are included in your concluding paragraph. For example *"As can be seen from the above there have been many criticisms of human rights law over a long period of time. Despite calls for reform of the **ECHR** and for replacement of the **HRA** little has been done in response to these criticisms. The whole area remains unnecessarily complex and case decisions are unpredictable. If the law is not clear and accessible people cannot achieve justice. Reforms are needed to make the law fit for the 21st Century."*

As with application of the law, you should try to take a logical approach. The beginning should introduce the subject matter, the central part should explain / analyse / consider advantages and disadvantages of it as appropriate, and the conclusion should bring the various strands of argument together with reference to the question set.

Where possible, try to consider alternative arguments. A well-rounded essay will bring in other views even if you disagree with them. Here is an idea of how you might structure an essay. This is only a rough guide; in the central part you will of course need to cover any specific issues raised by the question, e.g., a discussion of reforms, or of the development of an area of law, or of whether the law achieves justice.

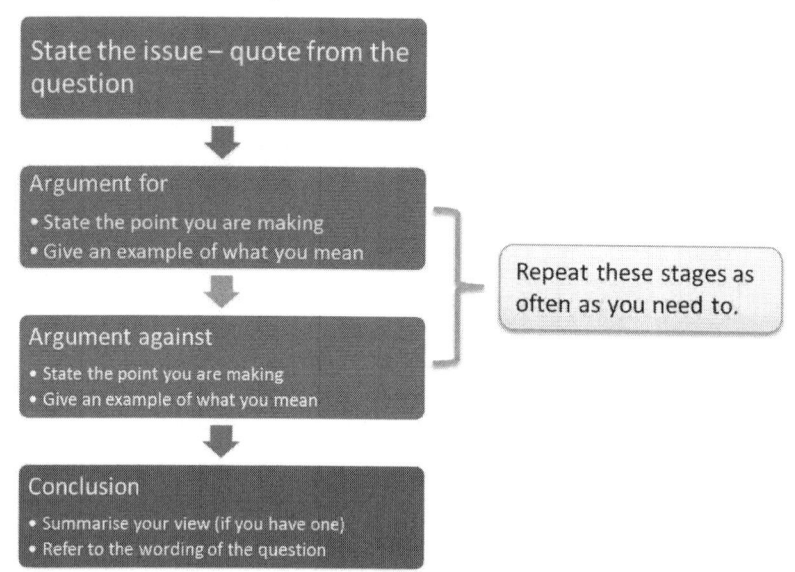

State the issue – quote from the question

⬇

Argument for
- State the point you are making
- Give an example of what you mean

⬇

Argument against
- State the point you are making
- Give an example of what you mean

Repeat these stages as often as you need to.

⬇

Conclusion
- Summarise your view (if you have one)
- Refer to the wording of the question

Task 40 evaluation practice

Look at the arguments for and against a Bill of Rights in the previous chapter. Select three arguments in favour of having a Bill of Rights in the UK and expand a little on each.

The OCR paper will not necessarily require you to link the law you have studied here with the nature of law. However, both topics are on the examination paper for Component 3 Further Law. In addition, Eduqas require evaluation of human rights in Component 3. I have therefore included the following from my AQA book and hope it may give you a few ideas for evaluating human rights law or for illustrating a discussion of the nature of law.

Extract from Human Rights for AQA A Level Law on links to the nature of law

The mixed questions and links to non-substantive law

The law spans various areas of process, procedure, rights and remedies and several different concepts, as well as substantive laws such as human rights, crime and tort. The topics you cover in your course are interwoven and you will need to show you understand the link between various areas of the substantive and non-substantive law. There are two mixed questions on each paper. Some questions may have a clear link although others may not. There will always be some type of link in these two mixed questions, however, so try to connect the two parts. One of the two questions is scenario-based, the other is not.

Example

A scenario may, e.g., involve the right to liberty and/or the right to freedom of assembly. This part of the question will ask you to *"advise X"* and you are likely to have to discuss the rules on police powers during your application of the law.

This could be followed by a question on the nature of law. This part of the question will ask you to *"assess"* the concept, e.g., asking you to assess how far these rules achieve a fair balance of competing interests or how far they achieve justice. You would explain balancing competing interests or justice and then use the rules on police powers to discuss how and whether a fair balance or justice is achieved. For balancing interests you would discuss the need to protect the public interest (in being kept safe) at the same time as ensuring the private interest is protected as these rights are important in a democratic society. For justice you would discuss whether the police powers are justified in a democratic society or whether they interfere with the individual's rights to personal autonomy and freedom of choice.

The concepts that are examined on the human rights paper are law and morals, law and justice and balancing conflicting interests. A question could involve topics within the English legal system or law-making, including the rule of law.

Before going on to the links, look back at 'The theory and nature of law for A-level' in Chapter 1 to remind you of the theories.

Links to the nature of law

Morals

There is a close connection between law and morality in human rights cases. Many of the **ECHR** rights have a moral base. Sometimes the law must get involved because a moral issue comes up in court and such cases often involve human rights. Euthanasia cases, withdrawal of treatment and medical advances as seen in **Quintavalle** are obvious examples. At other times it can be argued that the law should not be involved in moral issues. The case of **Brown 1994** went to the ECtHR where the decision in the HL was upheld despite the fact that it had been largely influenced by the judges' views on morality.

You could use almost any case on human rights to illustrate the connection between the law and morality because any protection of an individual's rights involves imposing a moral code on the state and public authorities. I have just given a few examples but have included each right. In each case you can say that there is no shared morality.

ECHR Article	Topic and moral connection	Case examples
Article 2 and 8	Withdrawal of life support and the sanctity of life under natural law conflict with personal autonomy and libertarianism	**Bland, Gard**
Article 2 and 8	Assisted dying and the sanctity of life under natural law conflict with personal autonomy and libertarianism	**Pretty, Nicklinson**
Article 5	Anti-terrorism laws and locking people up without charge is arguably immoral but opinion is divided on whether it should be illegal	**A v the Home Department**
Article 10	Blasphemy and obscenity may be immoral but again opinion is divided on whether they should be illegal	**Gibson**
Article 11	Freedom to protest is an important part of democracy but less morally justifiable if it is not peaceful or if the protest affects the rights of others	**Howell**

Justice

The above table can be used to illustrate justice, too. Human rights law is based on freedoms and personal autonomy. This connects to the libertarian view of justice because libertarians such as Mill suggested that justice should be allow for personal autonomy and as much freedom as possible as long as no harm was caused to others. The utilitarian view of justice, however, is based on maximising happiness for the greatest number of people. It thus focuses on the needs of society rather than the individual. It is in conflict with individual rights and freedoms and is criticised by libertarians, who see the rights of the individual as all important. This view of justice is concerned to improve the public good and has no time for individual rights which Bentham called *"nonsense on stilts"*.

The **HRA** and the **ECHR** increase the rights of individuals. This seems to be against the utilitarian theory, but it can be argued that society benefits from protection of everyone's rights. Therefore having these rights enshrined in law increases the greater good.

Anti-terrorism laws are arguably for the greater good of society. Detaining a person without charge breaches **A 5** rights, but a utilitarian may say that this is justified in order to protect society as a whole, i.e., the public interest and security. An alternative argument would be that society is weakened by going against the rule of law. The rule of law, like justice, requires fairness and access to justice. Such laws also go against natural law, as it seems immoral to imprison someone without a fair trial. A case example is **A v the Home Department 2005**.

In **Rogers v Swindon NHS Primary Care Trust 2006**, a woman took her local National Health Trust to court for not supplying a new drug shown to reduce the risk of recurrence of breast cancer. The court held the NHS to be wrong because her individual circumstances had not been taken into account. This type of case is an example of how distributive justice applies in practice and connects to economic theories of justice.

A utilitarian would want the hospital resources distributed to provide the greatest benefit for the most people. This could mean not giving expensive drugs to one patient, but instead using the funds to give more people a chance of a cure, or a better quality of life as long as this achieved the maximum happiness overall. Marx would want any such distribution to depend on the needs of the patient. Rawls would probably prefer an egalitarian approach, so that resources were shared more equally. The problem with achieving justice under any one theory is that resources are limited so not everyone will be satisfied.

Balancing competing interests

All human rights law involves balancing competing interests between the state and public authorities and the individual, i.e., public against private interests. Some rights involve balancing different private interests. These are covered in Chapter 6 so I have not repeated all the cases. For an explanation of rights look back at Chapter 1 and ensure you can explain claim rights and freedoms and the views of Hohfeld and Pound. Then consider how far the law has to balance interests using case examples. Here are a few ideas outside those showing the conflict between **A 8** and **A 10** covered in Chapter 6.

Examples

The state has to protect the public as a whole but at the same time has obligations under the **ECHR** to protect individual rights. There will inevitably be a conflict in such cases. This can be seen in **Brogan v UK 1988** and **Roberts 2015** in respect of rights under **A 5**. **Laporte 2006** is an example of the conflict concerning rights under **A 10** and **A 11**. Other conflicts arise between the right to life under **A 2** and the law on murder and assisted suicide seen in cases such as **Purdy**. There are plenty of other examples seen in Chapters 3, 4 and 5, especially where police powers are involved. In such cases there is often conflict with individual rights and also with personal autonomy and the freedom to be allowed to have a voice in a democratic society.

Examination pointer

Although justice, morals and balancing competing interests are linked to the human rights paper, AQA have confirmed that *"where appropriate, irrespective of the Paper to which a Nature of Law/ELS topic is assigned, examples may be drawn from the substantive law in other Papers"*. This means that, unless you have been specifically asked to discuss human rights cases only, you can also use examples from other areas to illustrate these concepts. There is likely to be a human rights focus, though.

Links to the English legal system and law-making

The topics from the English legal system and law-making that are examined on the human rights paper are the rule of law, delegated legislation, the European Union, the judiciary (including judicial independence) and access to justice. These involve procedural justice. This is also known as formal justice because it looks at the form rather than the substance of the law (hence also the term non-substantive law). Justice requires that there is a system of independent courts and tribunals for the administration of law and the resolution of disputes (what Professor Hart called *"justice according to law"*). This is a requirement under the **ECHR** and part of the rule of law. Procedural justice includes judicial review of a procedure or ministerial decision, i.e., of delegated legislation, the appointment and independence of judges, the financing of court cases and access to justice. Here is a little on each of these topics which are linked to the human rights paper along with the European Union. They are part of the rule of law too so we will look at that first.

The rule of law

This has been covered in detail in Chapter 1. Look back at that section and the connection to human rights (it is one of Lord Bingham's sub-rules). The ECtHR and the UK domestic courts have made clear that the rule of law is part of the legality requirement in **Articles 5, 8, 10** and **11**. Here is a reminder of that legality requirement for each of these rights.

A 5 provides that any interference with the right to liberty must be *"in accordance with a procedure prescribed by law"*

A 8 provides that any interference with the right to respect for a private life must be *"in accordance with law"*

A 10 and **A 11** provide that any interference with the right to freedom of expression and freedom of assembly and association must be *"prescribed by law"*

In each of these rights this legality requirement means that not only must there be a domestic law allowing the interference, but also that any interference conforms to the rule of law.

In **Beghal v DPP 2015**, the SC confirmed the legality requirement included conforming to the rule of law. This means any cases involving rights under these articles can be linked to the rule of law.

Lord Bingham also said that the arbitrary use of power went against the rule of law. Many cases involve challenges to the arbitrary use of power by officials (usually involving delegated legislation), e.g., **Hirst** and **Miranda**. The rule of law also requires independent scrutiny of decisions by officials. This involves having a system of courts and tribunals with independent and impartial judges. It also requires access to justice, including adequate funding of legal advice and assistance for those who need it.

Delegated legislation

Judicial review involves challenges to decisions and policies made by public authorities but not by Parliament. This will therefore be challenging delegated legislation. Public authorities are prohibited by **s 6 HRA** from acting incompatibly with the **ECHR**. A victim of such an act can bring a claim under **s 7** but there are lots of cases where judicial review is used as alternative. It is wider because a pressure group can bring a case on the basis of having sufficient interest in the matter, whereas under **s 7** only a victim can do so. Also **s 8 HRA** provides that damages are not usually awarded for cases under **s 7** whereas judicial review allows all normal English law remedies.

Judicial review challenges the form of the law not the substance of the law. It is a type of procedural justice rather than substantive justice. It is a way of correcting an injustice in the law by allowing people affected by it to challenge the way the law was made (Aristotle's corrective justice). That is why the cases are in the style of *"R on the application of"*. R is for Regina, the Queen, who represents the state. The state brings the action on behalf of the applicant (the person affected). It is common to reduce the name to just refer to the applicant and the department or minister being challenged, e.g., **Purdy v DPP** or even just the applicant where there is a long case name.

The European Union

The **Charter of Fundamental Rights of the European Union** (commonly called the **EU Charter**) includes all the **ECHR** rights so there is a strong link between the two areas of law.

In particular, **A 7** of the **EU Charter** is the equivalent of **A 8** of the **ECHR**. The case of **Watson** was brought under **A 7** but exemplifies **A 8**. Similarly, in **Google v Vidal-Hall 2015**, the case was brought under **A 7** but was decided on the basis of the English law on misuse of private information. In **NT1 and NT2 v Google 2018**, the HC again considered misuse of private information, but this time the claim was based on **A 8 ECHR**.

Both the **ECHR** and the **EU Charter** allow the state a margin of appreciation to avoid rights where necessary in the interests of public health or security. This is another similarity between the two.

N.B: It is a common mistake to refer to the Council of Europe as an EU institution but it is not. Although the Council of Europe works in close partnership with the EU it has no role in European law making. It was formed prior to the introduction of the **ECHR** to uphold democracy, human rights and the rule of law. All signatories of the **ECHR** are members of the Council of Europe but not all are members of the EU.

Judges and the independence of the judiciary

There is an overlap with the rule of law which requires that there is a fair system of courts and tribunals. Here is a reminder of one of Lord Bingham's sub-rules.

Adjudicative procedures must be fair. This means open court hearings, the right to be heard, the right to know what the charges and evidence against you are, that the decision maker is independent and impartial, and that in criminal cases D is innocent until guilt is proved. Fairness would also cover access to justice and appropriate help with funding a case.

Another link between the judiciary and human rights is that a court is a public authority so must comply with **s 6 HRA**. This means a judge's decision can be challenged by way of an appeal or a judicial review if it goes against the rule of law.

Independence of the judiciary is important because the **ECHR** encourages judges to be active and to take a purposive approach to interpretation of domestic law. The ECtHR has referred to the **ECHR** as a living instrument which needs to evolve. If judges are thereby changing the law it is vital that they do so objectively and without bias. It is also important that they are independent from the state because the state is usually the defendant in human rights cases.

However, a judge cannot overrule an Act of Parliament, only make a declaration of incompatibility, so this keeps the judiciary from being too active. Case examples include **Bellinger** where the HL ruled that the state law was not compatible. The law was later changed by an Act of Parliament. In **Miranda**, the UK court issued a declaration of incompatibility with **A 10** because there were inadequate safeguards against the arbitrary exercise of the power. Situations where there is arbitrary use of power and inadequate independent and impartial scrutiny will be against the rule of law.

Access to justice

Access to legal advice and representation has been seriously reduced under the **Legal Aid, Sentencing and Punishment of Offenders Act 2012 (LASPO).** The bill took a long time to get through Parliament but was finally passed. The arguments against the bill were that any system of justice should be based on equality and that if people felt they could not get access to justice they would not believe in the rule of law. However, the Minister for Justice argued that although legal aid is *"an essential part of the justice system"* the money has to come from taxpayers and resources are limited. This means balancing competing interests. The shadow justice minister said that any system of justice should be based on equality. This is a matter of distributive justice and raises the question of whether there is a fair balance of benefits and burdens. In all human rights cases all domestic remedies must be attempted before a petition can be made to the ECtHR. This is time-consuming and expensive. The **HRA** has improved matters as, since it came into force in 2000, applicants can rely on the rights under the **ECHR** in the domestic courts. However, there are many occasions when the domestic law cannot be reconciled with the **ECHR** so any challenge will have to go through the appeals system and then to the ECtHR. If legal aid is not available this may be impossible. The reduction in access to legal advice may also affect **A 5** because without proper advice a suspect may be kept in custody longer than necessary.

It is also important in relation to **A 10** as lack of access to the courts due to financial constraints would indirectly be an interference with a form of freedom of expression, the freedom to bring or defend a claim.

On a more positive note, the **ECHR** only requires the court to award just satisfaction and **s 8 HRA** supports this. This means an award of damages is not the normal remedy and even if damages are awarded they are unlikely to be excessive (merely just). This achieves a fair distribution of burdens and benefits and ensures that individuals and organisations are not restricted from expressing themselves purely because of the fear of a huge settlement being granted to the other party (a particular issue with defamation cases). In this case freedom of expression is supported.

There are no answers for the next two tasks but you should do these before you try the examination questions.

Task 41

Look back at the criticisms in the previous chapter along with the evaluation pointers. Make a few notes on the problems with the law and the difficulties these pose for both claimants and judges. You could add a little on how you could use these issues in a discussion of e.g., justice or balancing competing interests. Keep these notes for revision of both human rights and the nature of law.

If you are confused by a case, or you see cases which conflict, make a note of them. You can use these cases to illustrate an argument that the measure under scrutiny does not comply with the rule of law or does not achieve justice. If there is confusion or uncertainty then there will be a valid case for arguing that the law is not fully satisfactory. Justice requires clarity in the law and clarity is also part of the rule of law, so any ambiguity will go against this rule.

Task 42

Look back at any of the tasks that you had trouble with. Do these again and then check your answers before attempting the examination questions.

Examination question practice

Task 43 application question

After breaking up with her boyfriend Heather discovered she was pregnant. She wanted to keep the child but her parents made her have an abortion because she is doing her A-levels and they want her to have a decent career. Her father, Ted, is a well-known advocate of moral values and an active anti-abortion campaigner. He does not want the public to hear his daughter had an abortion. He picked her up from the clinic but as they were leaving Boris, a local photographer, used a long-lens camera to take secret pictures and says he will sell them to the press with a story about her abortion. Heather wants to prevent Boris passing the pictures to the local paper. Ted is also concerned that the government might use the pictures in their campaign literature on recent proposals for liberalising the abortion law as he is known to be against this. Boris has already posted some of the pictures on Facebook.

Consider what rights and remedies Heather and Ted may have under **Article 8** of the **ECHR** in respect of the pictures. **25 marks**

Task 44 application question

The government propose bringing in a law to prohibit the sale of all cigarettes and tobacco products. There has been widespread opposition but many favour the ban. Two main groups have formed called Let us Be and Tobacco is Death. The leader of Let us Be, Ellie, organised a march to oppose the ban, having given notice as required by s 11 Public Order Act 1986. Members of Tobacco is Death marched alongside shouting and chanting and displaying posters showing pictures like those used on cigarette packets to shock. Although Let us Be marched peacefully there are some instances of pushing and shoving by the Tobacco is Death groups which look like they could turn nasty. The police order Ellie to abandon the march and get her members to leave the area. She said the group had a right to march and had been doing so peacefully. The police respond that there is likely to be a breach of the peace caused by the Tobacco is Death group so they have the right to order the group to disperse. Ellie eventually agrees but says that Let us Be will hold a further march followed by a meeting to demonstrate against the ban.

Having regard to the ECHR consider the legality of the actions of the police in relation to the march and whether they can prevent the planned march or demonstration.

Assess the extent to which the rules you have applied achieve a fair balance of the competing interests involved. **25 marks**

Task 45 evaluation question

Examine the provisions of the **Human Rights Act 1998** and how they affect English law. Discuss how far the rules may be criticised and whether there is need for reform. **25 marks**

Index of cases

A v B 2000 .... 88, 91
A v the Home Department 14, 46, 62, 120, *See* A v the Home Department 2005
A v the Home Department 2005 ...... 14, 46, 120
ADT v UK 2000 56
Al-Khawaja 2009 50
Al-Khawaja 2011 50
Andrew v MPC 2017 .... 54, 69
Austin 36, 39, 40, 44, 45, 46, 61, 81, 82, 117, *See* Austin v UK 2012
Austin v Commissioner of Police for the Metropolis 2009 36
Austin v UK 2012 .... 36, 61
B v UK 2004 56
Barbulescu v Romania 2017 57
Beatty v Gillbanks 1882 .... 23, 60, 81
Beghal 47, 48, 53, 59, 80, 81, 122, *See* Beghal v DPP 2015
Beghal v DPP 2015 .... 47, 122
Bellinger 55, 96, 103, 123, *See* Bellinger v Bellinger 2003
Bellinger v Bellinger 2003 55
Benham v UK 1996 25
Black v the Secretary of State for Justice 2015 .... 54, 56
Bland 12, 38, 120
Bland 1993 12
Brogan v UK 1988 .... 46, 121
Brown 1994 .... 12, 14, 119
Campbell 70, 71, 74, 80, 87, 88, 89, 90, 94, 96, 97, 100, 109, *See* Campbell v MGN 2004
Campbell and Cosans 1982 25
Campbell v MGN 2004 .... 70, 90, 96
Cheshire 96, *See* Cheshire West and Chester Council v P 2014
Cheshire West and Chester Council v P 2014 36, 40
Christie v Leachinsky 1947 39
Collins v Wilcock 1984 39
Commissioner of Police of the Metropolis v DSD and another 2018 28
Conway v SS for Justice 2017 54
Cossey v UK 1993 55
Davis 2008 .... 50, 51
Dickson v UK 2007 56

DPP v Jones and Lloyd 1999 82
DSD and another 2018 95, *See* Commissioner of Police of the Metropolis v DSD and another 2018
Evans and another v Alder Hey Children's NHS Foundation Trust 2018 38
Evans v AG 2015 15
Fadeyeva v. Russia 2003 56
Ferdinand v MGN Ltd 2011 .... 87, 91
Foye 2013 51
Gard 57, 103, 120, *See* Gard and others v UK 2017, *See* Gard and others v UK 2017
Gard and others v UK 2017 57
Gaughran 2015 69
Gemmell & Richards 2003 12
Gibson and Another 1991 78
Gillberg v Sweden 2012 59
Golder v UK 1973 .... 25, 103
Goodwin .... 62, 63, 103, *See* Goodwin v UK 2002
Goodwin v UK 2002 .... 55, 74
Google v Vidal-Hall 71, 80, 100, 123, *See* Google v Vidal-Hall 2015
Google v Vidal-Hall 2015 .... 71, 100, 123
Greens and MT v UK 2010 94
Guzzardi 37, 39, 40, 45, 46, *See* Guzzardi v Italy 1980
Guzzardi v Italy 1980 37
Hashman and Harrup v UK 2000 80
Hicks 44, 45, 61, 62, 63, 67, 103, 117, *See* R (on the application of Hicks and others) v Commissioner of Police for the Metropolis 2017
Hirst 27, 29, 32, 63, 93, 94, 97, 101, 102, 103, 109, 122, *See* Hirst v UK 2005
Hirst v UK 2005 27
Horncastle 2009 .... 30, 33, 50
Howell 1981 .... 45, 82
Howlett v Holding 2006 73
Ibrahim and others v. the UK 2016 50
Ireland & Burstow 1997 73
James v UK 2012 37
Joseph v Spiller 2010 72
Kaye 24, 78, 79, 80, 87, *See* Kaye v Robertson 1990
Kaye v Robertson 1990 .... 24, 78, 80

126

Kennedy 59, 76, *See* Kennedy v Charity Commission 2014
Kennedy v Charity Commission 2014 .... 59, 76
Laporte 83, 98, 121, *See* R (on the application of Laporte) v CC of Gloucestershire 2006
Leander v Sweden 1987 59
M v A Hospital 2017 54
Maguire 2018 51
Malone 24, 68, 94, *See* Malone v Commissioner of Police for the Metropolis 1979
Malone v Commissioner of Police for the Metropolis 1979 24
Malone v UK 1984 .... 24, 94
Mengesha v Commissioner of Police of the Metropolis 2013 64
Middleton 2016 .... 89, 91
Miller v Jackson 11
Miranda 59, 62, 65, 80, 81, 97, 102, 103, 122, 123, *See* Miranda v Home Department 2016
Miranda v Home Department 2016 59
Moos 44, 61, 82, 98, *See* (on the application of Moos) v Commissioner of Police for the Metropolis 2012
Moos 2012 61
Murray 11, 71, 88, 90, 91, *See* Murray v Express Newspapers 2008
Murray v Express Newspapers 2008 ..11, 88, 91
Murray v the UK 1996 37
Murray v UK 1996 .... 51, 116
Nicklinson 120
Nicklinson & Another 2014 54
NT v Google 73, 89
NT1 and NT2 v Google 2018 .... 71, 123
Observer and Guardian v UK 1991 .... 78, 103
Ostendorf 39, 40, 45, 103, *See* Ostendorf v Germany 2013
Ostendorf v Germany 2013 37
PD v CC of Merseyside Police 2015 64
Peck v UK 2003 .... 55, 57
PJS v NGN Ltd 2016 .... 89, 91
Ponting 1985 77
Pretty 12, 74, 120
R (Gillan) v Commissioner of Police of the Metropolis 2006 .... 17, 42, 101

R (on the application of Hicks and others) v Commissioner of Police for the Metropolis 2017 44
R (on the application of Laporte) v CC of Gloucestershire 2006 83
R (on the application of Moos) v Commissioner of Police for the Metropolis 2012 44
R (on the application of Nicklinson and another) v Ministry of Justice 2014 104
R (on the application of Pretty) v DPP 2002 .. 12
R (on the application of Purdy) v DPP 2009 74, 99
R (Roberts) v Commission of Police of the Metropolis 2015 42
R v R 1991 13
R v Secretary of State for the Home Department Ex parte Kwawaja 1984 ... 16, 23
Re A 2001 .... 11, 13
Rees v UK 1986 55
Reynolds 2001 72
Roberts 42, 43, 57, 63, 121, *See* R (Roberts) v Commission of Police of the Metropolis 2015
Roche v UK 2005 58
Rogers v Swindon NHS Primary Care Trust 2006 121
Sheffield City Council v Fairhall and others 2017 92
Steel v UK 1998 45
Sugar v BBC 2012 76
Sunday Times v UK 1979 25
Thompson and Venables 1999 .... 25, 49, 51
Trimingham v Associated Newspapers 2012 . 73
UMO Ilinden 60, 61, 63, *See* UMO Ilinden v Bulgaria 2012
UMO Ilinden v Bulgaria 2012 60
V v Associated Newspapers and others 2016 .... 88, 91
Viscount St Davids 2017 79
Von Hannover 55, 59, 87, 90, 91, *See* Von Hannover v Germany 2012
Von Hannover v Germany 2012 .... 55, 90, 91
W v Secretary of State for Justice 2017 56
Watson & Others v Home Secretary 2018 68
Weller 90
Weller v Associated Newspapers 2015 .... 88, 91

Printed in Great Britain
by Amazon